To UPKAR

WITH PLENTY OF

GOOD WISHES!

(misfit)

[signature]

andreas
souvaliotis

misfit

changemaker
with an edge

Misfit: Changemaker with an Edge

Library and Archives Canada Cataloguing in Publication

Souvaliotis, Andreas, 1963-, author
    Misfit : changemaker with an edge / Andreas Souvaliotis.

Issued in print and electronic formats.
ISBN 978-0-9920295-0-0 (pbk.).—ISBN 978-0-9920295-3-1 (pdf).—
ISBN 978-0-9920295-1-7 (epub).—ISBN 978-0-9920295-2-4 (mobi)

1. Souvaliotis, Andreas, 1963-. 2. Social entrepreneurship.
3. Entrepreneurship—Social aspects. 4. Social change. I. Title.

HD60.S68 2013   658.4'08   C2013-904319-5
                                          C2013-904320-9

Copyeditor: Barbara Kamienski
Design and production: Joseph Gisini/PageWave Graphics Inc.

Published by Andreas Souvaliotis
www.misfit-thebook.com

Printed and bound in Canada

4 5 6 MI 17 16 15

thanks

To my unique parents,
for gifting me with almost unlimited airspace.

To my little brother,
for redefining brilliance and helping me grow.

To Justin's dad, the only friend and teacher I never met,
for inspiring me to be so creatively different and so Canadian.

To Danielle Crittenden and Kerry Harris,
for nudging me so effectively to tell the story.

To my editor, Barbara Kamienski,
for wrapping my thoughts and words so masterfully.

And to my beautiful Joe,
for shaping me in every imaginable way.

contents

foreword

Storytelling has always been one of our species' simplest but most beautiful and effective developmental tools. We share and show and guide one another through our stories. Stories help us find how to belong, they help us learn faster and they so often help us leapfrog over a moment of self-doubt or pain.

Andreas's very human story ignites a range of emotions as you travel through this unique memoir. You feel his bewilderment as a marginalized and oddly gifted kid; you shudder sympathetically for an isolated gay teenager in a society that wasn't quite ready for him; and you definitely feel his overwhelming excitement about arriving, discovering, creating, and succeeding in a new world that embraced him so openly.

His message is straightforward and powerful: harness the things that make you different in order to change your world for the better. We're all misfits, with our own particularities. And, in our quest to fit in and live "normal," we too often quash those very things that could make us special.

Andreas is a changemaker. By caring enough and by not being afraid to be different, he became one of our country's more outspoken, passionate and recognized eco-entrepreneurs.

His inspiring, colorful, and uniquely Canadian story will hopefully entertain you, spark your imagination, stretch your appetite for life and multiply your desire to stand out and contribute to your tribe.

— Justin Trudeau & Sophie Grégoire

why

I am different. I have always been different. I grew up scared of being found out, scared of my natural inability to fit in, to conform, to look and sound and dress and behave "normal." I was always drawn to the different ones and I observed them in total fascination—but the thought of being even a little bit like them totally mortified me. I was desperate to fit right in.

It took me a very long time to grow up. That relentless pursuit of "normal" continued to dominate my life until not that long ago. My fear of being found out ruled over my childhood, my adolescence, my twenties, thirties and most of my forties. I was terrified of rejection and I always linked any form of it (from bad customer service to losing an employee to fighting with a lover) back to who and how I was. I stretched myself all the time so I could blend in and found all that effort exhausting and demoralizing. And nothing ever really changed (I felt): I fit in as little at forty-five as I did at five.

But then something remarkable happened: I call it *audience response*. As my life and career took an unexpected turn in my mid-forties, and as I wrapped all my passion around a cause, I suddenly found my own voice. I stood on public podiums, wrote for newspapers and magazines, debated with big thought leaders and politicians, preached to followers and employees and discovered an enormous fuel source in me. Not only did I stand out, not only was I different, more passionate, more outspoken, more intense, more bizarre and much more controversial than those "normal" people on the other side of the podium—I was also less afraid than they were. It was incredible: one day I was (or at least thought I was) the biggest lover of convention and conformity—and the next day I was carrying a flag and didn't even care to count how many were actually following me.

It all happened in a flash. On a beautiful spring morning in 2007, sitting in my backyard and licking my wounds from a spectacular career derailment, I came up with a big idea—and I found myself contemplating the most daring and unconventional pursuit of my life. My strange genes had already helped create a thousand jagged edges in my career trajectory, but nothing had come close to the wild turn I was about to take.

At a time when others were still trying to figure out that new "green" thing and understand how climate change would reshape the business world, I accidentally became one of the earliest eco-entrepreneurs in my country. I invented something completely new, triggered a mini-revolution within my industry and inspired all sorts of brilliant minds to follow me on a wild journey. I blended my deep passion for climate with everything I knew about influencing human behavior and dreamed up a way to change our world a little bit by simply rewarding people when they made responsible choices. Somehow, maybe by pure luck or maybe through weirdly wired brain advantage, I landed on that idea before anyone else—and it ultimately became my legacy and my source of endless appetite for disruptive innovation. The dream and the venture snowballed for years, and along the way I grew into a natural and very public evangelizer, proudly sharing the tale of how magnificent it is to stumble into that magical intersection of passion and skill. I had finally discovered my very hidden and very particular ability to bring a little bit of change to the world, my world.

My story isn't especially profound. I am not a psychologist, and this book contains absolutely no scientific theories or facts; it's just a simple human case study. It is the story of how an erstwhile geeky and paranoid kid suddenly, and almost by accident, discovered his real purpose in this world, and how that enabled him to repurpose the sum of his unique attributes—eccentricities, skills, fears and passions—into a changemaker's toolkit. Once the realignment had begun, the rest happened quite naturally.

Nor is my story unique. Every one of us has what it takes to trigger a bit of change in the world; the only difference is that some people know this, and others mistakenly believe that their being "different" is a handicap. It is not. And so I offer you my quirky story in the hope that it may inspire you to discover and trust your own capacities.

numbers

MARCH 1969

S	M	T	W	T	F	S
						1
2	3	4	5	6	7	8
9	10	11	12	13	14	15
16	17	18	19	20	21	22
23 30	24 31	25	26	27	28	29

WORLD'S MOST EXPERIENCED AIRLINE

They gathered all the students in the schoolyard, and then my Grade 1 teacher took me by the hand, walked with me up to the small balcony and started telling all the kids how incredible it was that their young schoolmate had just been on TV. My face felt really warm and I kept touching all the funny powder that had caked nicely onto my cheeks and forehead. I squinted in the bright sunshine and tried really hard not to look back at all the pairs of eyes staring at me.

It was March 1970, and I was six years old. My dad had just driven me back to school from the Greek national TV studios, where I had been interviewed live by the host of a popular weekly program called *Stories You Wouldn't Hear in the News*. A friend of a friend of the family knew him and had told him about this young kid, living in a middle-class suburb of Athens, who was strangely skilled at memorizing calendars. So he sought me out and brought me onto the program. Back then television in Greece was still quite primitive; everything was broadcast live (in black and white, of course) and absolutely nothing could be recorded or edited. I remember the host discussing this with my dad while the makeup crew were working on my face, asking if I would be able to perform my "tricks" under that kind of pressure, and I remember my dad reassuring him that nothing fazed me.

Two years earlier, when I was just four, my dad (who worked for Air Canada in Greece) had brought home one of those classic desktop airline calendars. That little triangular cardboard treasure instantly became my best friend. I loved all the black and red numbers, and once I figured out that all the Sundays were marked in red, I began to try to make sense of all the patterns. My mom had already taught me how to read and understand numbers because I was taking piano lessons. Like all good airline calendars back then, it also spilled into the first two months of 1969, so I started to notice some interesting patterns: the same date in two different years was actually a different day of the week; and while in 1968 February had twenty-nine days, in 1969 it had only twenty-eight. I was completely mesmerized, kept asking questions and couldn't wait till the fall, when my dad finally brought home the brand-new 1969 calendar! Now having both years in black and red in front me was like magic. I sat for hours learning all the patterns and differences between the two years, and I began to memorize and compare all the days in red: for instance, in April of 1969 the Sundays were the 6th, 13th, 20th and 27th, whereas in the same month the previous year the Sundays had been on the 7th, 14th, 21st and 28th. In my own primitive way, I had just learned how to tell what day of the week it would be (or had been) on any date, going back or forward as many years as I wanted! I didn't need any more triangular desktop calendars: All it took was memorizing fifty-two red numbers and learning when and how to add or subtract one or sometimes two days of the week to the previous year's calendar. None of it ever overwhelmed me; it all made totally simple sense and, of course, I didn't understand why that was such a big deal for grown-ups or how I ended up in that TV studio. (I just wish they had kept a recording of the show!)

Things only became more numerically interesting and complicated as I grew up. Numbers consumed me, talked to me, actually made more sense to me than words and truly described the world to me. I relied on simple patterns to memorize countless phone numbers, car license plate numbers, weather statistics, track and field scores, car engine displacements and anything else that popped up in front of me. I would reinvent board games like Monopoly, much to my friends' frustration, by adding sales and income taxes, complex lending interest structures or anything that could satisfy my endless appetite for numerical stimulation. I aced math in school, and I developed a massive weather tracking project, which required that my parents buy me increasingly sophisticated thermometers, barometers and hydrometers so I could have more and more detailed figures to record, track and compare. When my parents moved homes, a few years after I left for Canada, my mother accidentally tossed out a huge box full of binders with all my weather stats—and I actually held a grudge for a very long time.

Once my brain was wired that way, it was impossible to unwire it, so numbers continued to follow me and talk to me right through my life. Time and basic social maturity gradually helped me conceal some of my "numerosis," but digits and their relationships continued to dominate my brain all the time. Not surprisingly, my undergraduate degree was in mathematics and computer science, and it was one of the easiest accomplishments of my entire life. My accountants have always dreaded me. Our friends' kids run and hide when I start asking them math questions. And my fascination with weather and climate gradually morphed into a much more serious study of climate change, which eventually formed the seed of my social cause.

When my mother died, I noticed the first incredibly tragic pattern of numbers in my life: I noticed that my mother's entire life and death were defined, or perhaps almost predicted, by two basic digits (2 and 3) and their two single-digit products (6 and 9). Take a look at this:

* My mother was born in '39.
* She died in '99.
* She died on the 23rd day of the month.
* She died 36 days after her initial heart attack.
* She died 9 days after being discharged from hospital.
* My dad was 69 years old when she died.
* She was 60 years old.

- They had been married for 39 years.
- I was 36 years old.
- She was 23 years old when I was conceived.
- I was born on the 9th day of the month.
- I was born in '63.
- She was 26 when my brother was born.
- My brother was born on the 23rd day of the month.
- She died in my home, at 99 Harbour Square.
- My phone number at the time was 203-6666.
- My spouse's phone number at the time was 932-9962.
- Both her parents had been born on the 3rd day of the month.
- My mother's mother died on the 9th day of the month.
- My mother's sister was born on the 9th day of the month.
- Both of my mother's siblings married people born on the 23rd day of the month.
- The sum of the digits of my mother's birth date (27/02/39) is 23.
- The sum of the digits of her only sister's birth date (09/09/41) is 23.
- The sum of the digits of her only brother's birth date (18/01/49) is 23.
- (And, for some extra goose bumps, the *only* two other people I know whose birth dates add up to 23 are my spouse, Joe, and my very special friend, Summer Graham, who was actually born on one of the most numerically perfect dates: 23/06/93).

That's how I've always seen the world.

notes

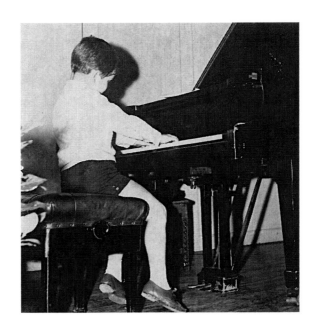

One of my dad's childhood friends became a well-known Greek musician and composer. His name is Mimis Plessas, and his fame and success spanned almost the entire second half of the twentieth century in Greece. Both he and my father were big lovers of jazz through their youth, and they were both gifted with excellent musical ears, but Mimis was the only one who ended up training in music and ultimately making a career out of it.

When I was four years old, in early 1968, we were at a restaurant one day with Mimis and his family. As was often the case, the grown-ups were teasing me with all sorts of well-known songs, and I kept singing along with them. I had been singing a lot since I was a toddler, and my dad was so proud of my apparent skill that he had actually been making reel-to-reel recordings of my songs since my first birthday. Mimis, obviously impressed by the way I kept up with their tunes, grabbed a carafe, poured water into a bunch of glasses on the table, handed me a spoon and then asked me to try to "play" a particular song by clinking those half-filled glasses. I took the spoon, tested all the different glasses, put them in the right order in front of me and then quickly started to build the song we had been singing a few moments earlier. Around the table, jaws dropped, and I remember Mimis leaning into my dad's ear and whispering to him for quite a while. Then he got up, walked over to my side of the table, hugged me, held me, looked into my eyes and said, "My little Andreas, you will become a big maestro some day."

As fate would have it, our two families ended up vacationing in the same beautiful fortress town in southern Greece (more on this later), so he and I would spend our summers together, going on boat rides, snorkeling, swimming, singing on the beach at night, talking about music and about the world. He was much more than my dad's old friend—he was my very own big, wise, fun, funny, sweet and caring life teacher and friend. I felt proud whenever I saw him on TV or heard him on the radio, and I remember marveling at how perfectly he spoke not only his native Greek but also English. In those early years, he called me "maestro," and that made me feel very special. Later on he switched to calling me *glaraki mou* ("my little seagull"), because he had once helped my brother and me rescue and nurse an injured seagull.

That very first glass-clinking concerto ended up changing my entire life. On Mimis's advice, my parents sought out one of the best-known piano teachers in Greece and quickly plunged me into lessons, at the ultra-tender age of four and a half! I couldn't read yet, so my mother had to quickly help me learn numbers (essential for reading notes and hand positioning). I was too short to be able to reach the piano pedals for many years after that, so I had to learn to play and sustain sounds without them. Although I was much smaller than any of the other kids I would sometimes see at my teacher's studio, none of it made me feel strange: I just enjoyed all the attention and loved being able to use my fingers to create beautiful sounds from that very big instrument. I didn't even mind all the pressure and the fact that within a couple of years I had reached the level where I had to practice piano for four long hours every day!

My teacher was the same well-known woman who had once taught piano to my mother. Her name was Katy Mavromichali, and she was an older, rotund, sophisticated, strict but gentle aristocrat from Istanbul (descendent of one of the well-known Greek families of Constantinople from another time). I instantly became her favorite, and she started to heap all sorts of attention onto me. She made sure I was always her last student each Wednesday evening, so she could have the freedom to stretch our time together, while my poor mom kept worrying about having to rush home with me so she could then help my little brother with his homework! Katy was incredibly demanding; I remember showing up at her studio and feeling the same kind of intense anxiety each week, expecting her to make plenty of critical comments and find all kinds of mistakes in whatever I had practiced. And yet, at the same time, she was warm and affectionate: She always had special sweet treats for me, always kissed me hello and goodbye, always asked questions about my school, my friends and our family vacation. She had no kids of her own and, as the years wore on, she started to proudly describe herself as my surrogate mom.

Katy was well connected in the classical music community in Greece and knew how to push a kid to advance very quickly in that space. My first public performance took place before I had even turned seven. My first appearance on television was no more than a couple of years after that. My repertoire was exploding with each passing season, and I was quickly competing against kids ten years older than me. Beyond what Mimis had discovered with those half-filled water glasses, my teacher was able to confirm early on that I was actually gifted with what's known as "perfect pitch"—the ability to not only hear and understand the relationship between different musical notes but also instantly and correctly name every single note I heard, anywhere, anytime. Car horns, squeaking doors, chirping birds, airplane engines, phones, door chimes, human voices—all of those everyday sounds were instantly translated into actual notes in my head. I loved being able to impress and mesmerize grown-ups so effortlessly and didn't comprehend why others couldn't actually do the same thing.

Yet, somewhere deep inside me, the seeds of resistance and resentment were already taking root. Four hours a day, every day (except Sundays!), was a painful commitment for a kid. I was expected to sit down at the piano at 5 p.m. each day and, apart from short bathroom breaks, wasn't allowed to leave the piano bench again until 9 p.m. By that time, all that was left of my day was a quick dinner and bedtime. As the years passed, my friends started going out to movies or to the soccer field—and I was still working away at the piano. When I asked (and later started to protest) about it, the answer was always the same: "You have an incredible gift, and you can't possibly waste it. When you grow up, you will realize why it was so important to work so hard and sacrifice so much at this stage in your life." And things would just continue the same with my 5-to-9 routine.

There were a few dramatic incidents along the way. I remember two in particular with a good dose of sadness, as both involved my mother.

Because my dad travelled a lot, it fell to my poor mom to ensure that I never slacked off; each evening, she was the one who watched and listened to make sure I didn't leave the piano bench for too long. Sometimes, if she had to leave the house for an errand, I would happily cheat and stay off the piano bench until the very last minute before she returned. But as long as she was in the house, even if she was napping (which was a standard Greek adult afternoon custom back then), she was always on guard and there was zero wiggle room for me. One afternoon, however, my grandparents showed up unexpectedly. I was very attached to them, and a visit like that was such a treat for me that, without even thinking about it, I stopped playing, sat on the edge of the piano bench and began to have a nice little chat with them while they waited for my mom to wake up from her afternoon nap. It never occurred to me, of course, that she was so conditioned to hearing me practice, even when she was asleep, that any but the shortest of interruptions would eventually wake her up. All of a sudden, she burst into the living room in her nightgown—clearly without her contact lenses and unable to see much past her own nose—rushed over to the piano bench, grabbed me by the ear, slapped me in the face a couple of times and yelled at me for being so irresponsible. The mayhem continued until her father jumped in to separate us. Only then did she pause, and turned to him to say (I'll never forget this), "Oh my God, what are you doing here?" I felt angry and embarrassed, but also vindicated in an odd kind of way.

The second incident had to do with my sabotaging one of the very strict rules imposed by Katy, my teacher. She was insistent that I never be allowed to practice without a metronome unless I was at the final stage of learning a piece, when I had truly reached performance mode—the "coloring" stage, as she called it, when it was time to combine all the technique I had learned with some emotion and expression. But until I got there, I was strictly forbidden to ever try to play so much as a single bar of music without a metronome! So one day, genuinely frustrated budding troublemaker that I was, I chose to toss my metronome off the piano and onto the hard floor, making sure it was completely broken. That way I had absolutely nothing to practice for the rest of that evening. Metronomes were not cheap, certainly not on our family's budget, and my poor mom ran all over Athens the next morning in order to find a new one. Not surprisingly, the new one didn't last very long either; a couple of weeks later, it too "fell" off the edge of the piano, but that was the end of my runaway to freedom. From that point on, the third and final metronome stood on a low coffee table, over a soft carpet, and I never skipped practice again.

With the arrival of adolescence and the flood of hormones it brought, my resistance and resentment multiplied rapidly. I had peaked musically around the age of twelve or thirteen because, even though there was still plenty of room to grow, I was quickly losing interest and I couldn't be bothered to apply myself to it anymore.

My music books were filling up with angry notations from Katy, "zero" marks and all kinds of other red ink. I became more and more tuned out and miserable; Katy became angrier and more disappointed over time; but my parents desperately hung on to the hope that once I grew up a little more, I would reengage on the road to musical stardom. By the time I was fifteen, I had started negotiating gradual reductions in the amount of time I was expected to spend practicing, and four hours a day eventually dwindled down to two and a half hours. Still, those 150 minutes each evening seemed like total torture. There was no escape. My parents' standard response each time I begged for permission to quit entirely was that as long as I lived under their roof, there was no other option: Music was my life and they would not let me throw away that gift. So I resigned myself to sitting hunched over the keys, all the while daydreaming and imagining what life would be like the moment I finished high school and moved away to Canada. How amazing it would be to have all that "found" time each day!

And then things got even more complicated. As I began to plan my big audacious move away from home and away from Greece and started to talk about going to the University of Manitoba for a science degree, my parents actually vetoed my choice! They were obviously crushed by my rejection of their dreams for me. Just imagine: Less than a half-dozen years earlier they had had a star kid on TV and in public recitals; they had spent every spare penny buying me the best piano lessons in town and the best books from overseas (not to mention replacing sabotaged metronomes); they had devoted so much of their own energy and time and passion over those fourteen years to help make it all happen—endless bus rides and taxi rides to the other end of town, just to make sure their gifted son got the best he could possibly get. They were living out an incredible dream of

27

their own, and now here was their pimple-faced, angry teenager announcing that he never, ever wanted to have anything to do with music again. A stalemate ensued: They absolutely demanded that I continue with music, and I flatly refused.

Thankfully, a wise old friend of the family from Winnipeg, Lillian Cholakis, who became one of my earliest Canadian mentors, intervened with a brilliant compromise idea: She convinced my parents to allow me to study whatever I wanted, as long as I went to a university with a strong musical culture where (hopefully) I could be indirectly influenced by those around me. The hope, of course, was that exposure to the right environment would somehow bring back all the magic and the passion for music. And thus came about the plan to send me to Brandon University, two hours west of Winnipeg in the middle of the Canadian prairies, just so I could be immersed in a school that boasted the second-best conservatory in the country. I had no idea what fun and bizarre times I was setting myself up for (but that's a story for another chapter in this book), so off to Brandon I went.

And then a funny thing happened: Not long after I had left my home, my piano and my 150-minute daily torture sessions behind, I actually started to miss it all. After just a few weeks in Brandon, I found a piano room in the basement of my dorm building and began to book it out, so I could go and play in the evenings. Then came the realization that I actually had something hot—word spread around campus that this new Greek kid was a really good pianist, and people started asking if they could come and listen when I played. And the rest, of course is history: As soon as I got my first job, I managed to scrape together $1000 and buy myself a beat-up old upright piano. Then I bought a better one, and an even better one after that, and I'll never forget the day that my first baby grand arrived in my condo in Toronto. I felt as accomplished as those grown-up kids who buy their first Harley!

One evening in the summer of 1988, when I was visiting my parents in Athens, they asked if I wanted to go to a wedding with them. The wedding was taking place at the Astir Palace Hotel, a famous resort on a gorgeous peninsula at the southern end of the city, and the setting for the reception was incredible—all outdoors, under the stars, with a dreamy view across the bay towards the city. I sat at a different table than my parents and just as dinner was about to begin, the staff suddenly rushed to my table and started rearranging everything to create room for one more guest. The new spot ended up being right next to me, and a few moments later the guest arrived: It turned out to be none other than Nana Mouskouri, Greece's biggest international diva of the 1960s, 1970s and 1980s! She had been living in Switzerland for many years, but she was in Athens on vacation. Her husband had just flown back to Geneva, and she was spending a few extra days on her own at the resort. As is the custom when a celebrity is staying at the same venue where a wedding reception is taking place, she was formally invited by the newlyweds to join their reception that evening; but that was just the polite thing to do and they hadn't really imagined that she would actually attend. Apparently Ms. Mouskouri, who had never met the couple before, had no better offers for that evening, so she decided to put in an appearance. As fate would have it, she ended up sitting right next to me, and as if that wasn't bizarre enough, I quickly discovered that she actually knew my mother! They had been meeting over the previous week at the swimming pool of the resort, because that's where my mother went to swim every day, and they had struck up a friendship. They were the same age and they spent a lot of their time talking about Canada, which they both loved. Somewhere along the way they started to talk about me; my mother told Nana how excited she was that I was coming for a visit and, of course, she proudly told her all about my musical talent. So when we she sat next to me and figured out whose son I was, she already knew plenty about me, and we ended up talking even more about my music. I was pinching myself. Really?! Having dinner and drinks and laughs with Nana Mouskouri?! And she's actually interested in me?! The more wine she drank, the more I drank, and the more prepared we both became for the surprise that came next.

At some point the band stopped playing and the lead singer announced that there was a musical celebrity among the guests: Would Nana like to join them on stage? Nana, who was several happy glasses of wine into the evening at this point, strolled up to the stage, grabbed the mic, thanked the band and the guests for the warm intro and announced that she would sing *only* if her new, young friend Andreas agreed to accompany her on the piano. Her new, young friend Andreas instantly felt the same kind of intense heat on his cheeks that he had felt twenty years earlier on that elementary school balcony, but obviously had no choice at this point—the guests were already cheering—so he got up, walked to the stage, sat on the piano bench in front of a few hundred strangers, and began one of the most unbelievable musical adventures of his entire life.

We played, and improvised, and laughed, and got more and more into it—instead of just a couple of songs, we kept going (glasses of wine in hand, of course) under the stars until almost five in the morning! My repertoire seemed somewhat broader and more diverse than hers, and at one point it looked as if she might run out of lyrics (there were no iPhones or online sources of lyrics back then!). This is when my over-enthused father came to her rescue: He got up, joined us on stage, and whispered the lyrics into her ear. It quickly turned into the Souvaliotis+Souvaliotis+ Mouskouri clown show! At some point, in our scramble to come up with even more songs, I asked her if she could sing anything by Billy Joel. She looked at me and said, "Wow, Billy. I haven't talked to him in so long . . . I wonder how he's doing." I was still pinching myself!

That was the start of a quirky friendship with Nana. After that, whenever she came to do a concert in Toronto, she would ask how many friends I wanted to bring along—the first time I was obnoxious enough to ask for sixteen tickets. We all ended up going out for drinks with her after the concert, and my friends were in total disbelief as she chatted with them about their lives and signed records for their moms!

There have been all sorts of other fun and special encounters with well-known musicians through the years and many other crazy musical feasts along the way. One of the most memorable ones was twenty years after the impromptu concert with Nana, in the spring of 2008: I was in Sydney, Australia, for a conference, and Joe and I were invited by a friend to a private, middle-of-the-night tour of the enormous pipe organ at the Sydney Opera House. My friend had actually paid some money to the man who had originally installed that pipe organ in the opera house, just so he could let a few of us musicians and music lovers check out that majestic instrument when the place was closed. We walked into the huge, dark opera house at midnight and climbed the tiny spiral staircase up to the organist's perch; then our tour guide switched the organ on, and we suddenly had the world's largest pipe organ, inside one of the most famous performance venues in the world, literally at our fingertips. He actually encouraged us to try it, and I remember playing songs by the Beatles, Elton John, Billy Joel and even some from the Phantom of the Opera and making that huge opera house reverberate. It was truly unbelievable.

Through it all, however, it's still been tough wiping out some of the complexes and hang-ups that piled up during my very intense fourteen years of music training as a child. To this day,

I still have a really tough time playing on command; it sort of makes me feel used, in a weird kind of way, and I almost freeze up. I definitely play easier and better if I've had a couple of drinks— a lot better, in fact, according to my spouse! But I do play and I do enjoy it. It's taken me a long time, but music is finally now becoming just a beautiful, unique hobby, nothing more than the distant echo of a very intense defining phase in my life.

roots

I was that happy kid in that special happy bubble, the one who (secretly) believed he was luckier than anyone else. And it was all because of how I saw my parents.

My dad, Yanni, had a massive influence on me. He was the smartest, wisest, sexiest, coolest, funniest, most worldly, most sophisticated and most popular dad. My teenage girlfriends fawned over him. Their moms (and all the other moms) were totally intimidated by him and engineered all sorts of creative arrangements so that they could catch a ride with him to parent–teacher days at our school. Our teachers were afraid of him. We were afraid of him. My mom was afraid of him. And yet we all adored him, followed him, quoted him, imitated him and craved his attention and approval. My dad was really big, and his shadow was even bigger.

And yet, he really hadn't been born to be big. He was raised by a modest, shy, almost introverted father, a controlling mother and two older sisters during Greece's most miserable times around the Second World War. In German-occupied Athens and during Greece's civil war that followed, he grew up hungry and scared, with no real ambitions or plans for his future. He managed to finish high school but didn't study anything after that. He simply went into the army, as every young Greek man was required to do, and then life just happened: He liaised with the Americans who still operated military bases in Greece, improved his English and eventually found his way into the budding airline industry, first as a sales rep in Greece for a British airline and eventually as the manager of Air Canada's sales office in Athens.

He lived at home until he was married, at thirty, because that was really the only option he had. My grandmother was an exceptionally "in-charge" woman and she truly ruled over her children's lives—in fact, her grip was still strong right up until the day she died at almost a hundred years old. She was a special specimen of that final generation of Constantinople's Greek semi-aristocracy, most of whom were chased out of Istanbul by nationalist Turks after the end of the First World War. As a young single woman, she found herself in unsophisticated Athens in the early 1920s and spent the rest of her life feeling, speaking and behaving a cut above those around her—including her own husband. She "interviewed" her grandchildren's French-language nannies, entertained everyone with her singing and guitar playing at parties, terrified and terrorized us kids, cooked dreamy and exotic meals, had an opinion about positively everything and undeniably ran the lives of her entire extended family. I remember sitting at her dining room table, as a teenager, watching her examine my father's fingernails and lecture him about the way he cut them!

He lived safely under her apron until he married my mother—and spent most of the rest of his life balancing between the two very different estrogenic poles in his life. He had also been shaped by his two older sisters. The eldest, Toula, quickly set the bar very high for the rest of the family: In the misery, chaos and poverty of wartime Athens, she decided she would become a doctor, and began to chase her dream with single-minded determination. She specialized in anesthesiology, managed to become the first female anesthesiologist in all of Greece, married her very successful and much older mentor, quickly amassed some serious wealth, became a widow at a very young age, married another prominent doctor, built up even more wealth and eventually, well into her seventies, retired from medicine, sold her private clinic and dove headfirst into her even bigger passion in life, becoming a famous playwright, poet and author in Greece by the age of ninety! My dad's other sister, Poppy, was a stunningly beautiful woman, sophisticated, kind, warm—the real soul of that family. My dad looked up to both of them in incredibly genuine but complicated ways, and his entire personality, marriage and life-style were heavily influenced by these women.

Even though he had no formal education beyond high school, he had the depth of a scholar and the exterior of a lecturer. He read and opined and debated all day long. There was no topic on which he didn't have strong views: from economics to religion to politics to nature to relationships to human sexuality, it was all his domain and he loved shaping his listener's views. His job as an airline manager gave him two basic staples: a necessary income for his family and a semi-glamorous platform for his exploits and discoveries. He travelled as much as he could, so he could learn, meet, play, eat, drink and enjoy life to the max. Having been raised in such an intensely controlled environment, he had obviously hit on the perfect career. Even as a married man with grown-up kids, he still regularly lied to his mother about when he was supposed to be back from each trip, just to give himself a bit more breathing room and avoid her phone calls on his first day or two back in town. Although they had no financial headroom whatsoever, he and my mother would take advantage of every possible business trip to tour the world in fairly glamorous style on his employer's coin. Sometimes they would take us with them—and then we would instantly become the talk of our school, particularly in a country as poor as Greece in the 1970s, for jetting off to Rome or London or Vancouver a couple of times a year—but most of the time they would go off on their own. In the very early years, in fact, when air travel was still a bit scary, they would travel separately and meet up in Hong Kong or Nairobi or Lima—so if anything happened at least one of them would survive to take care of us!

But all that adventure and excitement still wasn't enough for my dad's voracious mind. He needed deeper and more complex stimulation, so at a fairly young age he became a Freemason and rose rapidly through their ranks. Eventually he blended his Greek nationalist passion with his Masonic philosophical appetite and became a prominent international representative and lecturer on behalf of the Freemasons of Greece. He thrived in that environment of constant debate, regular bouts of controversy, fairly complex politics and plenty of fame and recognition for him as an unlikely leader in that space. It became his cause and his passion.

Growing up right at the core of a young, immature and unstable democracy also brought some interesting political threads into my dad's life. One of his first cousins was a leading communist during Greece's civil war in the late 1940s and was eventually jailed and exiled. His other first cousin married a senior army officer who ended up leading the infamous 1967 military coup and becoming a senior participant in the notorious junta that ran Greece until the mid-1970s. He was accused and convicted of all sorts of crimes after the junta was toppled and spent the rest of his life in prison. (By interesting coincidence, he died on the day that I was writing this part of the book.) And as if that wasn't enough political spice and drama in the family, one of the best-known political murder victims of the past century in Greece was the brother of that famous old doctor who had mentored and married my aunt Toula; he was a very popular, outspoken socialist in the early 1960s, and it was widely rumored that the CIA was behind his murder, a few months before I was born in 1963. (In fact there was a popular American movie made about his life and death, called Z—pronounced "zee"—which sounds like the expression meaning "he is alive" in Greek.)

So that was my dad's world. It's what made him so complicated, wise, ambitious, scary at times, sexy in just about everyone's eyes and remarkably deep. He was also a very talented guy, but had never enjoyed real opportunities to properly exploit his talents. He had an unbelievable musical ear, which, of course, made him my absolute terror whenever I practiced piano near him. He was also a superb photographer and a sharp writer.

Not surprisingly, he spent his twenties dating countless women, many of whom ended up knowing each other, because his world in central Athens back then was so tight and intertwined. Things never became particularly scandalous, but he always had lots of entertaining stories from that wild and playful era. And then, one day, he met my mother. She was barely twenty years old (he was almost thirty), had certainly lived a lot less than he had, but she felt confident enough to take him on. And within a year they were married.

My mom, Fofo, was totally different from my dad. She was shy, artistic and had been raised in a much milder, quieter, uncontroversial family. They had arrived in Athens only a few years earlier, as part of a mass exodus of foreigners from Egypt. Brits, Greeks, French and Italians had been the top colonizers of Egypt for generations and had enjoyed disproportionately comfortable lifestyles as the ruling class of that country. But the Egyptians began to stir after the Second World War, and the 1952 revolution was the beginning of the end for many of the resident minorities. Along with hundreds of thousands of other Greeks, my grandparents packed up the family and moved to Athens the following year. In a flash they went from being part of the ruling class to having to blend into a society that felt a lot less refined than their foreigner "club" culture in Cairo. Egyptian-Greeks spoke and lived differently than Athenians, and most of them ended up forming their own cliques in their own separate suburbs of Athens. My grandfather continued to work for a Greek bank. My mom and her two younger siblings found it easier to adjust, and they quickly started to thrive in their new hometown. The three kids grew in quite different directions. My aunt Haris grew up to become a very well-known architect, specialized in

Byzantine architecture and spent most of her career designing and restoring historical homes, together with her husband, in the very special walled medieval "castle" of Monemvasia in southern Greece. My uncle Nasos moved to England, became a marine engineer, married, had kids and stayed there for the rest of his life; he and I almost grew up together, in fact, because we were so much closer in age.

My mom finished only high school and then started working an admin job at the American military base in Athens. That's how she met my dad. Their families seemed to get along right away, perhaps because they were mostly expats, and the whole thing came together quickly. A month or two after the wedding, my dad got his first airline job and my parents started to explore the world. They waited four years before having kids, mostly because they had the time and the appetite for fun and travel—but also because they didn't have the money! When I was born they were still living in a tiny apartment in the center of Athens, which I think was costing them the equivalent of less than $30 per month!

My brother, Nikitas, came along a year and a half after me. He was smaller and very different from me. He didn't really speak until he was three or four years old. He was a lot less social or expressive than most kids and when he started to go to school, his special needs became much more apparent: he had trouble connecting with other kids, he required a lot of handholding just to keep up and the teachers began to offer a range of suggestions to my parents about what was going on. The general consensus was that my brother had developmental challenges and that he should repeat one or two grades in order to properly catch up.

My poor parents, in the absence of any real expert opinions, began to stubbornly fight back—because, despite all of my brother's social skill challenges, they could tell he was actually a smart kid with no basic intelligence gaps. So they were confused but also convinced that everyone else was wrong, and they stubbornly pushed him ahead. It took three more decades and a whole bunch of scientific progress before my brother's condition was finally diagnosed as Asperger's Syndrome (high-functioning autism), so unfortunately, and just like millions of other Asperger's kids around the world, he was raised with the pressure of having to live and learn and talk and adapt like every other non-Asperger's kid.

It was a rough and strenuous ride, for not only Nikitas but also the rest of us. My mother quit her job and dedicated a huge part of her time to him. Both she and my dad armed themselves with the sharpest and most convincing arguments and stories about why their two sons were so different from each other; one was social (too social, perhaps), engaging and high-energy, while the other was shy, introverted and quirky, but both classic examples of how intelligence comes in multiple forms. Without realizing it, they were actually describing Asperger's syndrome. Of course, in their passionate resistance to having their younger kid labeled "retarded," they ended up accepting no further advice or expertise on what may have been going on with my little brother. It was perhaps not ideal, but nobody can ever blame parents for being genuinely protective and proud of their kids. The only unfortunate result of all that was the pressure and the stretching that Nikitas had to endure right through his formative years—just because everyone's goal was to make him just like everyone else.

Over time, my parents' relationship began to suffer under the pressure and strain of having to fight off society when it came to the massive differences between their kids. My mom's domain was gradually reduced to just her home and a kid who really needed her. My parents' trips together became shorter and less frequent. By the time she was forty, my mom had started to develop a dependence on alcohol (although it took us a lot longer to figure it out), and my father had started to tune out.

They became edgier and older than their age. There were still lots of beautiful family moments and plenty of real warmth and affection between the four of us, but the two of them were really tired and not particularly healthy. My mom smoked and drank heavily and started to have very strange blackout episodes (sometimes even falling and hurting herself), which we were eventually able to link to an extreme acquired sensitivity to alcohol. I remember coming home from a high school party and finding her standing in the kitchen, totally unable to speak or even understand anything I was saying to her—and it felt just awful. Meanwhile my dad started to develop a severe case of psoriasis, which had a cascading effect on his overall health over time. It was so debilitating for him that he ended up having to be put on a permanent mild dose of chemo, which, as predicted, eventually wrecked his liver and killed him.

All that intensity actually translated into positive energy for me as a kid. I felt lucky. I enjoyed the contrasts and all the unique edges of our life as a family. Who else could possibly have jet-setting intellectual parents, infamous political convict relatives and famous high-achiever family friends? All that stimulation, positive or negative, was like a permanent adrenalin fix for me. It wasn't difficult to get hooked, and I grew up expecting more and more of it. Yet, at the same time it was also easy to feel seriously at risk of becoming an underachiever. I thought I'd never grow up to be as big as my dad, as cool as my mom or as successful as some of the others around me.

Even my brother's extraordinary skills in certain areas—his incredible photographic memory, for instance—would sometimes make me feel inadequate. Little did I realize back then that I might have also been growing up somewhere on the long tail of the autistic syndrome. Only decades later, when I finally had an opportunity to learn about Asperger's Syndrome and about the

41

countless possible shades and shapes it could take, did the blend of my own unique skills, my social awkwardness and my unbearable pile of insecurities as an adolescent and a young man start to make a little more sense.

school

I skipped kindergarten! I'm not sure why, and I never really asked. Maybe it had to do with my little brother's developmental challenges and my parents' anxiety about leaving him at home without his only sibling and friend for an entire year.

When it was time for me to go into Grade 1, I suddenly had a serious disadvantage compared to the other kids. I knew nothing about school and the social skills, desks and routines that come with it. I was totally lost and fit in so poorly that within a couple of painful months, I had to be yanked out of the gifted school where my parents had managed to get me admitted. I remember feeling a bit embarrassed and confused by all that, and I'm sure it was even more painful for my parents. I ended up in a school much closer to home and, after another couple of bumpy months, I finally settled in and started to thrive.

And the thriving lasted for twelve years, right till the end of high school. It was all so easy. The pace was too slow for me, and I would have easily become bored and difficult; thankfully I was kept busy and very challenged with my much more intense piano life. Homework was never painful. My inadequate or abnormal social skills made me a remarkably "unfiltered" and unedited keener: front row, hand up in the air all the time, eager to impress but also scared of all the mocking and the fun that the cool kids could (and increasingly, with the years, would) poke at me. I knew I was different, but most of the world was telling me it was okay, that I was actually only different in a good way.

Over time I learned to skim the tips of waves at school so efficiently that I actually became academically lazy. I really didn't have much of a choice, considering how little time I really had for schoolwork beyond my actual hours in school. As soon as I got home each day, I'd have to start on the piano, so that left very little time for homework. I rarely crammed but always did well—but I was certainly not developing any proper discipline.

I knew I had become the ultimate optimizer, and I actually bragged about it.

I was also becoming an optimizer on a different level: Because of my social awkwardness but also because I had been spoiled by my ability to maximize my returns with very little effort on the school front, I began to gravitate away from social situations that would stretch or challenge me. I didn't hang out with the other really smart kids in my class, because I couldn't be bothered to work as hard to keep up with them as friends. I wanted lots of friends, and my measure of success was definitely in the size of my herd—but it was all about optimizing in terms of quantity, not quality and depth of relationships. So I started to hang out with kids who weren't quite at the top of our class, like I was, or those who were actually younger than me, including all my younger cousins! It took my parents a while to clue in; for a while they just thought their son was such a generous soul, being friends with everyone and acting as a bit of a shepherd to the younger ones. But then eventually they started to notice the real pattern and they really worked hard—unsuccessfully—to change me. My mom used to mock me and call me "king of the little people." She used to tell me that I would never learn anything that way, but that didn't faze me; perhaps because that's all I could really handle. None of us realized it back then, but I really think I was already operating at the absolute limit of my social capabilities as it was.

Other interesting symptoms of my underdeveloped or weirdly developed social filters involved trust and sharing. In my eagerness to belong and to be appreciated, I wouldn't pause and measure anyone or anything (as most normal kids do): I would simply dive right in, throw whatever I could possibly find into a social situation and hope that my social generosity would earn me something. And this wasn't just when I was a little kid; this was my main, my known MO right through adolescence! No filters at all. If I liked you and wanted you in my life, I would immediately throw everything I had at you, from family secrets to invitations to spend the entire summer with us. I would come home and tell my mom I had promised my new friend Yanni that she would drive him to his German lessons. It was a constant fiesta of unfiltered trust and generosity, which drove my parents downright crazy—and their expanding paranoia about it drove *me* crazy with fear and insecurities.

By the time I went to university, I had so mastered my optimizer skills that I breezed through my undergraduate degree. Now I could even optimize the effort in advance, by choosing courses that I knew I could ace with little effort (in high school in Greece there had been no electives whatsoever). And on the social front, there was a great new twist to the previous "king of the little people" mode: king of the vanilla people! In Brandon, Manitoba, the exact center of the whitest and most uniform part of the country, I stood out like that giant single tree in the middle of the flat prairie. I didn't have to be cooler or more socially sharp—I just had to be me, with my weird accent, my funny name, my crazy stories about my faraway birth country. Without any effort and without needing to find a bunch of "little people," I was king again. It was an incredibly easy ride, even easier this time. By this time I had grown up enough to know what I was doing and why I was doing it, and the accumulation of all the easy-road childhood lectures from my parents had made me worry a bit more about the superficiality of my reign and whether I was actually learning or gaining much this way, but I was truly unstoppable. And, on reflection, I think I still learned plenty. I may have been clawing to the top of my social heap in unusual or unorthodox ways, but I was still succeeding—and I was learning exactly how to spot my niches and how to harness them.

gay

I remember the first time my dad said it to me. Then he said it again a few weeks later. And he kept saying it, in one form or another, for many years. It was that horrible line about how he would prefer to lose a child than to find out that his child was gay.

I remember my heart pounding in my chest each time I heard him say it. I remember the panic and the desperate hope that swirled in my head that somehow I had it all wrong, that somehow this attraction I always felt towards other boys was something that would eventually go away. I had to be wrong about it—because otherwise life seemed like an impossible dead end. I was utterly terrified of what was in me.

People always ask me how old I was when I first knew, and they expect to hear one of the typical responses from a gay man of my era: fifteen, seventeen, maybe even twenty years old. My answer, of course, is quite different and so much scarier: six, seven, or at most eight years old! I was a tiny, geeky, "gifted" kid when I first heard my dad say those ghastly words—and that's all it took. I knew instantly. I knew it with as much confidence and certainty as I do today. All it took for it to come to the conscious surface was that terrifying statement by my awe-inspiring father. It was the most crushing and revealing moment of my life. I was done. I was worthless. And I was maybe in Grade 2 or 3.

Greece in the 1970s was definitely a frightening place to be growing up gay; my dad was just an ordinary, progressive dad in that world. He was no more homophobic than his buddies or than a lot of my friends in school later on, but he was my god, the best and most intimidating communicator, and I had never doubted anything he said. So when that horrible line first came out of his mouth, it felt like the end of world for me.

Looking back, I think that this moment may have been one of the most useful turning points in my entire life. That realization of being different, of being alone, of having to compensate for what I thought was going to be a massive handicap, of having to manage and cover and navigate around my nature, all of that quickly morphed into incredible strength and skill. It was no different than what happens to those scrappy little kids who grow up on the street: they may be afraid at first, but they end up developing unbelievable layers of confidence and survival skills.

So there I was, growing up with this enormous and enormously premature secret. There were traps and scares everywhere, and I had to constantly manage. I worked really hard to change my feminine handwriting, to hide or eliminate all my expressive hand gestures on the piano, to speak differently, to play rough, like all the other boys in school. It was all conscious effort, all the time. And every time my dad would repeat some variation of that line, I would work even harder at it—and I would panic, thinking that maybe he was onto me.

I had a gay uncle and a gay teacher. They were both warm and caring, and my parents actually seemed to have a nice connection with them, but that didn't make me feel any better. They were grown-ups, I reasoned, so whatever little respect they got must have been because of that; as a kid, I must have been worth nothing.

By adolescence, the hormones were overflowing, the fantasies were overwhelming and the guilt was almost unbearable. As a ten-year-old, I had felt frightened because I knew I liked boys. As a fourteen-year-old, I felt trapped and terrified because I couldn't stop thinking about boys. I was ready to do something about it, no matter how huge the risk, and the only reason I didn't was because I couldn't quite figure out how and with whom. As confident as I may have been by this point in my own sexuality, I still felt like an extreme aberration and I thought that finding someone else like me out there would be next to impossible.

And then came my friend Makis. He and his family had just moved to our part of town, so he showed up in our school at the start of Grade 10. He and I hit it off right away—cool kid, smart, sensitive, good-looking and, by interesting coincidence, our fathers knew each other because they were both Masons. I latched on to that extra little secretive bond between us and kept building on it from there. In no time, this had turned into my first real infatuation and, because Makis was completely oblivious to it, he kept feeding it more and more fuel. We were hanging out all the time, chatting on the phone for hours, studying together and spending weekends away at friends' cottages. It was all Makis, all the time. And the pain and the hunger kept growing until I couldn't live with it anymore; even though I knew there was almost no chance any of this was mutual, I decided it was time to break my silence.

I remember the moment, as if it were yesterday. We were at his place and I asked him to go for a walk with me, so we could talk about something serious (I was too scared to have that conversation under his parents' roof). As soon as we were a couple of blocks away from his home, I stopped, looked him straight in the eye and said simply, "I really wanted you to know that I'm gay."

I felt as if I had just pushed myself off the edge of the highest diving board in the world. I did it quickly, without hesitation, but as soon as the words were out of my mouth, I felt as if I was twirling and tumbling through the air. I was terrified, but it was too late to shift my gaze, so, with the sun hot on my face, I kept looking straight at him. After only a few seconds, Makis locked eyes with me and, his voice totally calm, said, "Good for you, for trusting me with this. I am your friend."

So there it was: that earth-shattering first coming-out moment in a man's life. Except I wasn't a man—I was barely fifteen years old, and I had already lived with this for too long. The hormonally charged side of my brain might have been hoping for a different outcome from that exchange, but I really couldn't have gotten anything better from Makis. He wasn't gay, he wasn't interested in me that way, but he was my friend—and he was cool with it. That simple response taught me immeasurably much about life and the world that lay ahead: real and balanced friendships, the beauty of genuine revelations, the wondrous intertwining of trust and vulnerability in human relationships, the value of communicating and sharing confidently. All I was trying to do was express, and maybe even satisfy, my desperate hidden passion, but instead I got a fantastic first real lesson on deep human relationships. This was the defining moment of my adolescent years.

Makis and I drifted apart over time, and after high school we both moved to different corners of the planet and lost touch. It was only in our late forties, through Facebook, that we found each other again and I discovered that he actually lived just a short drive away from my godchildren, in eastern Australia! Not surprisingly, it didn't take me long to engineer a visit—and I felt extremely proud and blessed when, with that little bit of extra confidence that thirty years of adulthood had given me, I was able to raise a glass to him in his own home, in front of his wife, and thank him for that world-changing response to me a whole lifetime earlier.

The rest of high school was uneventful but still very troubling. I was alone. I was too driven and too hungry for life, and I couldn't just resign myself to being alone. So I started to think about moving to Canada. A few years earlier, Air Canada had come very close to transferring my dad to a new job in Edmonton, and in order to make that possible, they had rushed us, as a family, through the immigration process. In the end, the transfer never happened, but we were left with fully approved immigration visas—and the option of moving to Canada, either as a family or as individuals. I already liked Canada; apart from its wacky climate, which was a feast for my young, weather-obsessed mind, it felt like a good, fair, open, energetic and youthful society. In so many ways it provided the perfect fix for all my frustrations with Greek society, and it also offered me one other very simple advantage—distance!

My parents didn't object; in fact, they too really liked Canada and saw plenty of opportunity for their young, ambitious son (without having a clue about what was really pushing him away!). The distance didn't scare them, because they could fly across anytime they wanted for free, so they quickly jumped on board and helped me plan my big move for the summer of 1981, right at the end of Grade 12.

And off I went: fearless, restless, reckless, tireless and filled to the brim with energy to explore, to live and to build. It was an unbelievable high. It didn't matter to me where I was; I was just happy to have been unleashed onto the world, and I couldn't get enough of it. I showed up in tiny Brandon, Manitoba and created my own little hurricane in that town. I met all the local Greeks and convinced them to start a Greek school for their kids; I also started and anchored—with my new big Afro hairdo!—a weekly Greek TV news program on the local community channel; I got a job teaching piano to kids; and I acquired an army of new friends as well as a few boyfriends and girlfriends among them. The repressed and trapped little suburban kid from Athens was making up for lost time in so many ways.

I remember thinking that it was perfectly normal (and safe) in university to be dating both a local girl and a local boy at the same time—one was fulfilling my social "fitting-in" needs and the other was fulfilling everything else—until I was caught, of course! The girl turned out to be the boy's best friend, and because the boy was deep in the closet, I had never figured out the connection between them. Instead, they did, many months into our relationship(s), when I flew back to Greece for the summer and sent them identical postcards with identical messages ("I love you, I miss you, see you in September"). Mayhem ensued, of course, and in September I got back to Brandon only to find both of them standing in front of my dorm room and keen to have a very interesting conversation with me. Only then did this big-city kid start to realize that he was living in a much smaller fish bowl. The carnage from those first few years in Brandon was endless, but so were the memories and the beautiful growing up that came with it.

Through those early unleashed years, I actually stopped worrying much about what my parents thought or didn't think. I never wanted them to know, but I had also become a bit more careless, courtesy of the great physical distance that separated us. I would easily and creatively put my entire life on hold each time they came to visit, and I also became good about building the right safeguards during my playful summers in Greece. I thought that they considered their hyper kid a heterosexual Casanova, but this was naive thinking on my part. Slowly, very slowly, my tiny slipups, my mysterious patterns, my colorful friends and every-thing else in my whirling life started to synthesize into a pattern of suspicions in my parents' minds. And then came the big blow.

It was the 7th of October, 1985. I had already graduated and was living in Winnipeg with my brother and working as a very young computer programmer. After a short visit, our dad was about to fly back to Greece. It had been a bit of an awkward few days: He had made a few comments about my "faggy" friends and my weird clothes and slightly radical hairdo. With my thickened skin and life-devouring brain, I didn't really worry much. I kissed him good-bye that morning and went off to work. A couple of hours later, he called to ask if he could borrow one of my small suitcases because he had run out of space. "Sure," I told him. "Go into my bedroom, open my closet and take my blue Samsonite."

And that was it. In those few seconds, I had just unleashed the biggest scare in my young life and the biggest implosion in my relationship with my parents.

Inside the suitcase, he found an extremely revealing letter I had written to a boy months before and never delivered—and obviously forgotten about. I was done. Years and years of elaborate schemes and firewalls came crashing down in an instant. I was suddenly faced with the evolved version of my dad's horrible lines from the previous decade and a half. It was no longer about the choice of losing a child versus having a gay child. Now, with the choice already made for him, it was about him not wanting to be alive anymore. When he called me at work after he had read the letter, all he could say to me was that his life was finished and that I might never actually hear his voice again. Sobbing, he kept asking how I could do this to them and assured me the news would positively kill my mother. He said he hoped the plane taking him to Greece would crash, so he wouldn't have to ever see her and tell her about his horrible discovery. I sat at the other end of the phone, shivering and feeling as if my world had abruptly ended. That was one of only two moments in my entire life when I felt completely numb and totally paralyzed by fear (the other was just a few years later, when I happened to witness the public beheading of a convict in Saudi Arabia). I spent the rest of the day alone, terrified and with absolutely no survival plan.

And then the phone rang, very early the next morning. My mom was calling from Athens to let me know that my father had arrived, had shared the news with her and that she was packing her bags and flying out to be with me the next day. She sounded upset but not angry, and promised me that everything would be all right and that we would work together to "fix" the problem; she was already making arrangements for me to see someone about it. My paralysis was at once replaced with smiles and hope and excitement. The fact that she was still speaking to me—heck, the fact that they were actually alive and making plans!—felt like a huge gift to me, compared to how life had seemed when I went to bed the night before. I may have been cocky and hungry and restless and fun-seeking all these years, but I was still a scared little kid with the self-confidence of an average twenty-two-year-old, so I was ready to embrace any plan that could perhaps "fix" my biggest handicap in life. When my mom showed up in Winnipeg the next day and told me I was scheduled to see one of the best-known psychologists in town, I was on cloud nine—not in a logical kind of way, but just because. In that kind of extreme crisis mode, any escape path would do.

And so I went to see that psychologist and I remember being fascinated by how calm he seemed; the contrast between the two of us must have seemed hilarious to him! He opened by asking me why I was there. "Because I'm gay," I replied. His next question was whether it had been my own decision to come to see him or if someone had sent me. As soon as I told him it was my parents who had arranged it, he closed his notebook, looked me straight in the eye and said (I'll never forget this), "Alright then, we're done. It's actually your parents who need to come and see me, not you. Thanks for taking the time, and thanks for answering my question honestly."

What a weird mix of emotions! Was it a letdown? Was I actually hoping that a pro like him might have had some sort of magical solution for my "problem"? Was I just craving a friendly listener, someone who could untangle the unimaginably raw emotions I'd been experiencing for the previous few days? Or was I simply feeling vindicated? I drove home, shared the news with my anxious mom and then watched her implode. She pounded her fist on the kitchen counter, cried, swore and talked about how those "quacks" were all the same. Obviously, she never went to see my new favorite quack, but that moment marked the beginning of a very slow, often volatile, almost always painful but unbelievably important maturing in our relationship. The scrappy little kid had just inadvertently summited another huge mountain and was now finally ready to live an honest life.

It's amazing how much less complicated and tiring life becomes when you stop having to manage firewalls and personas! Most gay men and women of my generation seemed different and appeared to have quirky or complicated personalities precisely because they had to live differently than the rest of the population. They had to compartmentalize their lives and stories and affections. But once you remove that need, once you allow people to live open and honest lives like everyone else, then suddenly you find them growing up and living with far fewer quirks and unique complexities. I so wish that some day all gay kids will be able to grow up feeling as normal and as honestly integrated in society as I started to feel after that big and accidental revelation at the age of twenty-two. And I think that, in Canada at least, we're well on our way.

My life after October 1985 was so much simpler and more honest, compared to my life before. Suddenly it became about living, about absorbing and experiencing and sharing and loving, instead of managing, separating and packaging. My lifestyle could finally match my personality: I could dive, instead of hesitating and calculating; I could love, instead of being afraid; I could celebrate, instead of pretending. That incredibly scary moment of revelation was almost like a second birth.

It took a very long time for things to become truly comfortable with my parents, but I found the "work-in-progress" mode of our relationship quite stimulating. I didn't mind or fear their unpleasant comments anymore; I just saw an interesting challenge in them and sometimes entertained myself by trying to use a bit of shock therapy to shift their perceptions. As individuals, when they were apart, they would each try to accommodate and understand and adapt a lot more; but as a pair they were more difficult, because they habitually reinforced and supported each other's homophobic tendencies. Interestingly, they had automatically inherited my previous need for secrecy and compartmentalization. Now that they were in on the big secret, they treated it as their own—and they spent the rest of their years managing perceptions, questions, stories and assumptions among all their friends and relatives. Having been there in very painful ways through my formative years, I understood their pain, and out of respect, I didn't interfere. Because of that, some of my closest and dearest relatives didn't really know much about my life and didn't even get to know or love my Joe until after both my parents were gone. Once again, I know and hope that those who come after us will have it a lot better and easier.

I drew a huge amount of energy and inspiration from my newfound openness. In fact, I enjoyed becoming a bit of an early role model for others. When I got my first senior executive job in the mid-1990s, I felt uniquely proud that I was an openly gay leader in a fairly large organization—and I enjoyed having the disproportionate ability to help boost the confidence of some of our younger gay employees.

A decade later, when I was chasing my first CEO job, I spent a day with an industrial psychologist as part of an in-depth assessment and didn't hesitate at all to reveal the fact that I had a same-sex spouse (and that escaping the homophobia of my country of origin had been the main reason for my move to Canada years earlier). The psychologist didn't look at all surprised or uncomfortable, and I certainly ended up getting the job. A month or two later, he invited me out to lunch and shared two interesting things with me: Not only was he very surprised by what I had shared with him because, as he said, in all the years of assessing or coaching CEOs he had almost never come across another openly gay leader of an organization, but he also told me (in confidence, interestingly) the fact that he too was gay. We went on to become extremely close friends, and the two of us now share a mission to inject and inspire even more of that kind of openness into the corporate world. But I was still fascinated (and perhaps, secretly, a bit excited) by the fact that I was still on the absolute "bleeding edge" of our society's evolution as recently as ten years ago.

Shortly after that, I joined the Young Presidents' Organization, a global club of young CEOs that is perceived by many as a bit of a boys' club. I actually hesitated (for once!). I remember grilling the then chair of the Toronto Chapter, where I was being recruited, about that perception, and about how I would fit in. He responded with enthusiasm about how good it would be for the chapter to finally have a gay person join, and about how cool and progressive I would find the whole organization. And so I dove in, becoming the first openly gay member not only in Toronto but actually in all of Canada—more than 800 CEOs across the entire country and not a single gay man or woman until I showed up! It was interesting how quickly that tiny aspect of my DNA turned into a serious personal edge, in an organization that is so sharply focused on progressive leadership. Joe and I had suddenly found a perch from where we could really make a difference, just by being who we were and by naturally influencing some of the sharpest and most prominent leaders in our town and our country. We didn't have to say or do anything differently; we were having an impact simply by being there and quietly showing our fellow members (and, importantly, their kids) how being gay should be—and really is—of no consequence when it comes to a person's ability and opportunities to lead in our world.

home

I was born a nomad and a hunter. I escaped my home, country and continent because I was gay, but the beckoning distant horizon also teased me into doing it. My grandparents were immigrants, my aunts and uncles had moved or studied around the world and my parents lived on airplanes.

Nomads may be much more versatile and creative in their definition of *home*, but I think we also crave it more intensely and define it more deeply than most people. We attach a lot more feeling to it, and we may even derive a lot more satisfaction from its existence. And we can have multiple homes, or at least layers of homes that hold special meaning for us.

My first natural layer, of course, was Greece. I grew up in an acute love-hate relationship with my birth country: I loved the physical environment, the smells, the air, the light and the music. But I hated the way my compatriots thought and behaved, the intimidating "me-at-the-expense-of-you" culture, the unrefined laws of their jungle and the loud intensity of it all. I was always scared, and my secret isolation, particularly as a teenager, must have made that fear even worse.

By the time I moved to Canada, the negatives had almost completely overshadowed the positives, and I was elated to leave Greece forever. I didn't think I would ever miss it—and I couldn't have been more wrong. In no time at all, I found myself constantly and painfully craving the breathtaking sights and sounds and smells of that gorgeous country. The beautiful mountain I used to hike up all the time, with its crisp, dry wind; the overwhelming fragrance of the thyme bushes; the bright red soil under my feet; the brilliant blue sky above me; the salty smell of sea and the incredible feeling of that first dip into it, on the first warm day of spring; the food; the sound of young and old people playing guitars and singing "new wave" songs together late at night on the beach; the exquisite calm of bright summer mornings—such memories all added up to the most keenly felt homesickness imaginable.

As a kid, I actually had a couple of competing homes, and neither of them was my parents' rented house. The first of these was our little town of Papagou, which was just a bland, relatively new suburb of Athens. It had been first designed after the Second World War as a subdivision for military families but quickly morphed into a comfortable, distinct, uniform, middle-class suburb with its own eco-system of schools, markets, restaurants, movie theatres and parks. Papagou was at the eastern edge of Athens, right at the foot of one of the three mountains that wrap around the city. And our house was literally the last house on the edge of town, right at the foot of the mountain. I think my first real lover and friend was that mountain. I bonded with it from the time my dad used to take us on long hikes, but I really fell in love when I started exploring it on my own. I was always alone up there, and I never felt scared. I would hike huge distances, way up to the top and across the whole spine of it; every peak, every trail, every giant boulder had special meaning for me. The little bit of free time I had, outside of school and piano, I would devote to my buddy, the big mountain. One day I found a car that had been driven through a rocky trail and dumped at the bottom of a ravine, high up on the mountain; naively fearless as I was, I opened the door, found the registration, ran home and called the police, who quickly discovered that the car had been stolen a few weeks earlier. The stunned and grateful owners actually came to our house to meet and thank me for finding it—and they even brought me a gift!

My other real nest early in life was the magnificent "castle" of Monemvasia in the south of Greece. My mom's sister, as a young budding architect in the 1960s, had stumbled across it, and, together with her future husband, ended up making it the main project of her career and life. Monemvasia was one of the best-fortified medieval towns in that part of the world—perched on the side of a giant rock, right off the eastern coast of the Peloponnese. The rock was connected to the mainland by just a tiny causeway, hence its name, which means "single entrance" or "single access" in Byzantine-era Greek. Because it was such a tough place to conquer, over time it evolved into a uniquely diverse, multilayered collection of architectural styles from each of its occupiers through the Middle Ages. Venetian, Ottoman and Byzantine building treasures filled the entire town, but when my aunt discovered it, most of them were in ruins. By the middle of the twentieth century, a new town was blossoming across the causeway, on the mainland, and it was a much more convenient place for people to live, so all but maybe a dozen of the local families had abandoned the castle on the rock. The ruins of splendid old palaces, churches, mosques and schoolhouses were nothing more than worthless stones to the locals, and the only part of the town that remained standing was its beautiful walls. They wrapped around an astonishing blend of history, beauty, misery, poverty, ghosts and scorpions. Endless legions of scorpions thrived unchallenged in the ruins and under the piles of rocks. The place had no electricity, no sewage system, no shops, and there were no young people.

But my aunt and uncle instantly fell in love with the magic beneath that ghost town and started to imagine the rebuilding of an entire medieval city. They shared their dream and slowly let their passion infect government agencies, building code regulators, real estate investors and wealthy foreign tourists—triggering a gradual but magical renaissance that, over the course of half a century, helped recreate an entire historical town in the most authentic, respectful and meaningful way. Today, the castle of Monemvasia is a tightly managed, unique resort town, filled with impeccably rebuilt 500-year-old homes, spectacular boutique hotels, exquisite little restaurants and a distinct, wealthy and eccentric crowd of seasonal and, increasingly, permanent inhabitants. There are no cars, no roads, no lampposts, no power cables, no other outward signs of modern civilization—and there is no space, figuratively or literally, for mass tourism. It's one of my world's most special, sophisticated, deep and almost mysterious spots, full of thousand-year-old stories and ghosts. And, thankfully, the scorpions are almost all gone, victims of the legions of cats that came with the wealthy tourists and have happily thrived and multiplied in the protection of the castle's walls!

Charmed by my aunt's stories, my parents decided to take us there on a summer vacation when I was just six years old. Back then, with no power and many more scorpions than kids, the place felt a bit like a prison, but it wasn't long before Monemvasia's special energy drew us in. We went back the next summer, and then every summer after that. The "submarine atmosphere," as an old friend once described it, of feeling almost trapped together with everyone else inside the castle's walls quickly became one of life's sweetest addictions. In fact, one summer we literally got trapped in there: While the precious causeway was being rebuilt, a huge wind storm caused massive waves which quickly wiped out the temporary gravel bypass that had kept us connected with the rest of the world, and we found ourselves perfectly stranded in the castle. There was no way in or out, and the winds and waves were so ferocious that we couldn't even get food supplies delivered to us by boat. The whole thing probably lasted only a few days, but to us kids it sure felt like the most dramatic siege in the history of Monemvasia!

This was the second home that so deeply defined my childhood. It couldn't have been more different from my flat, vanilla, middle-class suburb in the big city, and I was inspired by the enormous contrast between my two worlds. Both of them shaped me in myriad ways—but Monemvasia really gripped my soul, as it did Joe's from the moment he first set foot there, many years ago. It is our mystical second home, drawing us back summer after summer, even from the other side of the world.

After high school, the intensity of the emotions and experiences around my escape from Greece and family made it all the easier for me to quickly define Canada as my new home. The contrast between Athens and Brandon could hardly have been greater, but within the span of only a few years, the quiet, simple, rural province of Manitoba had become my new, real home and left an indelible stamp on me. My real Canadian immersion took place in the social halls, murky rivers, blinding blizzards, flat farms and big, innocent smiles of the prairie world. I couldn't easily escape to anything familiar; the country of my origins was very far away. (And back then, long-distance phone calls were exorbitantly expensive.) Everything was completely new and different and thoroughly exciting for someone as hungry for change and validation as I was. My new world hugged me, nurtured me, liked me and—above all—respected me. That was more than enough for me to really fall in love, to dive in with all my passion and make it all mine. Manitoba will always be home, in the most meaningful of ways.

My move to Toronto in 1986 was also a bit of an escape. It had been less than a year since the coming-out drama with the family, and things were far from comfortable for me at home. My new, serious-for-the-first-time boyfriend, Dave, was decidedly unwelcome whenever one of my parents was visiting us in Winnipeg (which, because I was living with my brother and also because of everything else that had happened, was almost all the time!).

When my brilliant boss at work challenged me to find my way into an MBA program (more about this later), I purposely looked at business schools anywhere but Winnipeg. Eventually I settled on McMaster University, and Dave and I packed our bags and our cars and drove away to Toronto—for good! It was a bold move of defiance towards my still very tender and equally threatening parents; and it was also very, very exciting to be leaving my safe first Canadian "nest" province and heading into the intimidatingly busy core of the country. I remember the final couple of hundred miles, as we were approaching Toronto from the north on a typically muggy, hazy summer day: going from the cool, quiet two-lane country highway to more and more lanes of cars, more and more frenzy and noise, and heat and humidity and pollution! It felt entirely appropriate: big-city boy was returning to his busy roots, after having grown up so much through his five-year retreat in the Canadian hinterland. I was ready to do a lot more, live a lot more and immerse myself in a much faster race. That gradual increase of the pace as we drove down Highway 400 towards the big city was the perfect symbol of what lay ahead!

But Toronto didn't become home for a while. For the first several years, until long after I met Joe, my home was still under the big sky of Manitoba. I felt like a tenant in Toronto. I was good at using everything the big city had to offer me, and I definitely wasn't going to leave again, but it just didn't feel like home. From my mid-twenties until my late thirties I actually lived in the same building, on Toronto's Harbourfront, and loved the experience, the convenience, the views, the neighborhood, the busyness, the big wild parties, the real bachelor lifestyle. I lived big and fun. As I progressed in my career and could afford more, I kept moving up in that building, into more expensive and more impressive condos. My final act in that building was to move into a gorgeous and gigantic penthouse unit, way above the lake, with views all the way down to Niagara Falls.

I was proud of my sexy nest and energized by it—I spent a small fortune furnishing it and making it feel like the ultimate party pad—and then I woke up one morning and realized how weird it was for a single, busy, career-absorbed guy to be living in such an enormous space. I hardly ever cooked, I couldn't possibly cope with the hassle and stress of hosting dinner parties, and yet here I was, bragging about living in the ultimate entertainment pad. And of course my mind leapt straight to solution mode: Instead of regretting my expensive decision, I simply walked over to one of Canada's top chef colleges (which was within easy walking distance of the condo) and put up a bunch of notices on their bulletin boards, offering their advanced chef students free room and board in exchange for work as a live-in chef in my condo. Seriously! Before I knew it, my phone was ringing off the hook and the job candidates were lining up around the block. And bachelor-boy ended up with his own fabulous live-in chef, for absolutely free!

But no part of that incredible journey through my twenties and thirties ever really made me feel at home. Until something very special happened to me one night, in the company of the moon, high above Africa in the spring of 2001.

Just over a year earlier, my mom had died of a sudden heart attack while visiting me in my big Harbourfront condo. She was still young and cool and fun—and I was utterly devastated. In fact, her death changed me through and through. I had spent the year after her death wondering what really mattered in life, trying to reconcile all my new feelings and questions with my day-to-day lifestyle. I saw that I had fallen into the standard trap of the conventional immigrant to North America: jobs, money, lifestyle, cars, savings, retirement and more of the same. Why had saving money for retirement become almost more important than freedom today? Since when had spending more to look better and live better become an imperative, not a choice? I wondered how much convention had defined my mom's final years and how many different choices she might have made with her time if she had known she would suddenly drop dead at sixty. Would she have taken more than a week off work to go visit her kid in Toronto that year? Would she have conformed even less and done even fewer of the routine and required things that seemed to fill her life? Would she have spoken differently to Nikitas or me or even to our dad? Would she have drunk and smoked less—or more?! The deepened understanding of mortality that comes with the departure of a parent changed me forever—and inspired me to go back to how I once was, to how she once was. How would I like to feel if I knew I would die the next day? I dreamt of a whole different form of freedom, another level of strategic insubordination towards the rulemakers of human society. I still think that this abrupt wake-up call was the best gift my mother left me by dying so unexpectedly, so young and so close to me.

Project One was to bail on my career—and it sure felt like diving off the edge of the highest diving board! To the horror of my career-driven, conformist and conservative MBA buddies, I simply exited their world and threw myself into a year of discovery. I wanted to read, write, slow down, connect, ride my bike, get fit, get lazy, fall in lust or in love, enjoy my "home" and get to know myself. I could definitely afford a year of going "backwards" (by their horribly superficial and conventional definition), so I held my breath and took the plunge. No more glamor and paychecks and hundreds of employees. No more dull comfort, predictable alarm clock and drive to the office each day. No more ego-boost of feeling wanted or needed and no more empty-but-proud proc-lamations of being oh so busy. Now I would have time to write, to think, to inhale the newspaper cover to cover every morning at the neighborhood coffee shop, to cycle thousands of miles in a summer and to "waste" hundreds of hours on the beach.

But I started by jumping on a plane to South Africa, to meet my very special newborn goddaughters (much more on them later), and I purposely booked the type of ticket that would allow me to stop in Greece along the way to spend some time with my recently widowed and rapidly mellowing dad. After a few days with him in Athens, I took a quick side trip to the island of Crete, where we had made some fun local friends on a trip a few years earlier. At this point, Joe and I were just best friends and no longer lovers—we had officially declared the end of our romantic relationship nearly ten years earlier—so I showed up in Crete as a single, relaxed, unemployed, playful and willing dude from Canada. In no time, a fun little fling ensued with the gorgeous young brother of one of my hosts who happened to be in the Greek marine forces. And, perhaps predictably, the young marine was a bit upset when it was time for me to move on to South Africa. In fact, there were lots of questions as to why I wasn't extending my stay or why I wasn't at least planning to stop in Crete again on my way back to Canada, to which I replied (repeatedly) that I couldn't, because eventually I'd have to get back "home."

By fascinating coincidence, when I got to Durban, the same type of drama played out again: a beautiful little fling with the beautiful young brother of someone I knew there, with a similar torrent of tears at the end and questions about why I couldn't stay longer. And, once again, the same uncomfortable response from me: It was simply time to go "home."

And then came the fateful moment. My flight back left Johannesburg late at night and we headed north, right through the middle of Africa. I was sitting by the window, looking at the beautiful moon over the mysterious continent that had always fascinated me. Everyone around me seemed to be asleep, but I was awake and my mind was racing. All the fun of the previous few weeks: the lust, the discoveries, the endless appetite and then the scheduled separations and all those silly tears. Twice. And both times my lines were identical: I couldn't stay longer because I really had to get back "home." What was that all about? What was really drawing me back? Was it my town? My condo? My cats? My friends? My routines? Why the heck was I cutting short all the freedom and exploration that I had so daringly chased?

Maybe it was the moon or the special setting or the sweet loneliness of that moment, but something finally helped me get it: I had grown up! I had clawed my way a little higher up on Maslow's pyramid. "Home" was finally defined by love, not by geography or a lifestyle. It was a person, not a town or a penthouse condo or a job or a castle. Life had already presented me with my final, real and permanent home—and it was my beautiful lover, my best friend, whose soul had become so irreversibly intertwined with mine, even though he and I had spent the previous decade in such comical denial.

love

As a young kid, I always admired my parents. I thought they were the coolest, hippest, smartest and sexiest parents any kid could have. They were cooler than all my friends' parents: they spoke differently, they lived and looked younger, they travelled everywhere, they hosted really funky parties, they knew so much more and, above all, they seemed so uniquely connected to each other. Their remarkably tight emotional intimacy with each other fascinated and intimidated me. It seemed impenetrable, perfectly private and immensely powerful. At first I just admired it, along with everything else I admired about them. But over time, as my hormones began to flow and my insecurities began to explode, I started to envy it. I became completely convinced that I would never be as happy or as soul-connected to another human being as they were to each other. And that feeling of never being able to live as well and feel as fulfilled as those who had created me gradually became one of the heaviest weights on my soul and on my self-confidence right through the years of adolescence.

I never tried to rationalize that gap in my own expectations, and I certainly never talked to them about what it took to build their beautiful linkages; I just marveled and studied them in silence. But as my hidden envy blossomed, so did my childish attempts to invent my own circles of emotional intimacy. I would look at every new friendship as a potential opportunity for that type of magical mental connection with someone—and the excitement would drive me to overtrust and overinvest in every new connection with a human being without even checking for a hint of reciprocation. I would do the same with older relatives, aunts, uncles, even faraway family friends, whom I drew into becoming my pen pals. And I would write and phone and meet and talk endlessly, always hoping to find a way to feel as tightly connected to another soul as my parents obviously felt with each other. My teenage years were very clearly defined by this frenzied search for love and connections everywhere. I now see this as one of the strongest clues that I may share some of my little brother's blessed Asperger's genes. At the time, of course, my parents, and perhaps many others, simply saw me as a bizarrely hypersocial kid.

The sudden autonomy of my early move away from home opened up the range of possibilities but didn't change my style or momentum. I was still anxiously looking for love, still feeling quite deficient and deprived in that respect, but at least now I was a young adult, living unsupervised and feeling a lot more "normal"—because everyone around me also appeared to be hunting for the same thing. I enjoyed my enormous capacity to open up and invest emotions in new people all the time. I thrived on it, in fact. I loved the constant adventure, the thrill of discoveries and new forms of love and connection. I plunged, and plunged often, into the silliest and shallowest of flings and friendships. I learned to substitute quantity for quality and to bury my anxiety for emotional intimacy way beneath my frenzied "fun" lifestyle. I confused excitement with satisfaction. I drove myself so hard and fast and unearthed so many lust opportunities along the way that I managed to convince myself that I was riding the perfect wave. And, as I got into my twenties, the nagging sense of envy I felt towards my parents actually started to fade. The old folks started to look a little more tired, a little less perfect with each other and a little less inspiring—and from my high spot, right on top of that amazing wave, I started to feel as if I no longer needed to shift my eyes quite as far up to see them.

And then my entire world was reinvented. It was a gorgeous spring day, Mother's Day, the 14th of May, 1989. I was twenty-five years old and had just completed my second degree and started my first real job a few months earlier. I had finished cleaning up the big mess from a rowdy party I had thrown in my condo the night before for a couple of MBA classmates who were getting married. I was a bit hungover and sleep-deprived and probably not looking my best. But once the big cleanup was done, I had thrown on the cheesiest pair of red shorts and an ugly T-shirt and driven to Toronto's Greektown for lunch with a bunch of friends. We had sat on a patio and feasted on sunshine, garlic and laughs for hours. And then, as I was driving back home and feeling the lure of a hangover-induced cozy nap, I took an exit off the highway, parked the car and walked into High Park. I found an empty picnic table in the middle of a perfectly sunny, grassy field, lay down on it and fell asleep right away.

High Park was normally my favorite cycling destination: It was far enough from home to be a bit of a challenging ride, and its steep hills also offered some great speed and cardio thrills. I had always spent a lot of time cycling, particularly after moving to Toronto, with all its biking routes and paths along the lake. So on that beautiful, sunny Sunday, I was actually a bit frustrated at not being able to ride; my old bike was wrecked, and I hadn't yet figured out where and how to go buy a new one. (Not only was the thought of the astronomical $100 expense intimidating at the time, but I also didn't know how to bring a new bike home after driving to a store in my car!) So, showing up at the park in a car made me feel a bit envious of those with bikes, although all such thoughts were quickly eclipsed by my powerful sleepiness and the joyful prospect of taking a nap in the warm spring sun.

As I walked over to the picnic table, I didn't even notice that there was a person sitting at the next one, with a bike by his side. It was the only other table, and he was the only other human being in that entire grassy field, but I don't even remember seeing him. The whole time I slept, he stayed there. He just watched me, in my geeky clothes, my day-after-the-debauchery tired and ungroomed face and my very own little Greek-meal garlic cloud hovering above me and keeping the mosquitoes away. And then, when I finally woke up (still unaware of him sitting at the table behind me), he suddenly asked me if I had the time.

In my well-trained hunter's mind, that was the most eye-roll-worthy pickup line. But hunters, of course, can't miss opportunities, so I turned to him, told him the time (it was twenty minutes to seven) and for the first time noticed his beautiful face and his really genuine look. I remember thinking instantly, *How did I miss that before?* We started to chat. We talked about cycling. (I discovered that he almost never biked—how odd was it that he would be there on his bike on a day when I was there without mine?) We talked about Greece (he had been there a couple of years earlier and had even learned a couple of impressive tongue twisters). We talked about parents, family, our recent degrees, Toronto, the weather, jobs, just about anything. We kept talking for what seemed like hours.

And then it started to get dark and cool, and I started to worry about how he would cycle all the way home from there—or maybe I was looking for a reason to continue talking—so I offered him a ride home. He refused, just because he couldn't imagine how to fit his bike into the tiny trunk of my car, but I kept insisting, of course. Eventually, with three-quarters of his bike sticking out of the back of my car, we slowly and very carefully drove to his parents' home. When we got there, he offered to meet me again someday and help me go buy a bike; his sister had a hatchback car. I found a piece of paper in my car (a gas station receipt!), wrote my numbers on it and sealed my fate.

That was the most important and defining day of my life. The incredible human being who wrapped his soul and his endless love around me, who ended up becoming my real and only home, who has shaped me so deeply and in such meaningful ways was sitting there, on a lonely picnic table, right under that glorious sun, just waiting for me to walk right past him, not even see him and fall asleep in front of him. And, as he always does, he just waited. He wasn't hunting for anything (or ever, really), and even I, the relentless hunter, wasn't after anything that day either. We both just happened to be there, accidentally sharing the same love for that same gorgeous spring sun. That day and those two lonely picnic tables turned out to be the time and place for the most magical intersection of two people's lives.

We fell in love right away. We expressed it and addressed it in different ways and at different times, but we were both drawn in really fast. The journey was complicated right from the start. Hyper hunter meets sensitive mellow novice. Spoiled, determined, autonomous, hungry career builder courts shy, ambivalent, protected, family nest boy. The wondrous intensity and magic of what we felt for each other were tested, day after day, by the opposing forces in our lives and lifestyles. My parents never really accepted him. His beautiful parents didn't even need to accept me, because for the longest time they didn't know what was going on.

A few years into it, we actually thought we had separated. We were so in love with the love we were feeling for each other that we wanted to find a safe and cautious way to protect it from being torn up by the daily trials and tensions of our intense relationship and our different circumstances. So we came to the brilliant decision that we would no longer be lovers—we would just be best friends. We told the world about it, and nobody seemed to believe us, but we convinced ourselves and pretended to be single for almost a decade. The hunter went back to his familiar ways and the sensitive mellow novice tried to learn how to hunt as well.

We spent ten very funny years in complete denial. Our friends kept laughing at us and making bets on how long it would take for us to stop pretending and come back to our senses. It really was impossible to unwrap the most perfect blend of two human beings but, somehow, we held on to the assumption that our hybrid existence was all we needed. We lived and dated separately but never let a single day go by without speaking with each other; we could travel only together; our lives overlapped more and more and more—not out of habit or need, but out of want. We felt everything I used to envy about my parents' soul connection and it was right in front of our eyes, but for ten long years, we tried to pretend it wasn't really there.

And then, finally, on that late-night flight over Africa, came that moment of recognition. As it all came together, my brain started to rage with a wild mix of intrigue, relief, happiness and positive anxiety. There was so much I suddenly had to tell Joe, but I was trapped inside a plane at forty thousand feet, ten thousand miles and twenty-four hours away from home. I jumped up and asked the flight attendant for some writing paper; all she could find were a bunch of small airline notepads. I sat for hours in the quiet, dark cabin, my tray table illuminated by the tiny reading light, and shared my big *aha* with the love of my life on seventeen small, loose notepad sheets. I pretended that we still had a choice, that we could still choose to build separate lives and somehow maintain a special friendship with each other in the background. But it was obvious from the way I wrote that we didn't have a choice.

By beautiful coincidence, by the time I landed back in Toronto it was the 14th of May—the twelfth anniversary of that very unintended pickup line in High Park (an anniversary we always celebrated with a lot of smiles and gratitude, even in our most "single" years), so it was the perfect moment for me to deliver the letter. I asked him not to read it until after I had left his apartment—and then he stayed up all night and cried. Exactly 365 days later, on our thirteenth anniversary, we announced to everyone that they had all been right, all along, and we had only been pretending. (Thirteen, of course, has always been Joe's favorite number, and now it's ours.)

Everything I admired, envied and craved as a kid, an adolescent and an insecure young adult, I have been lucky enough to have. I am comfortably, genuinely and confidently in love, and I've had the good fortune to have lived that way for almost my entire adult life. There's such a magical, mysterious core underneath the multiple layers of our beautiful connection, and that's the source of my contentment and confidence as a human being. The fact that I belong, that I have such a fundamental emotional nest is perhaps the most energizing aspect of my existence. Joe and I have an expression that perfectly encapsulates the simplicity and the depth of fulfillment we draw from life: We look at each other, at random and totally ordinary moments, and just say the words "happy days"! And by doing that we constantly remind ourselves that any average day with each other is plainly happy. Being so united, so mysteriously connected and so inseparable is a pure and powerful source of happiness.

Not many years after Joe and I met, I made a couple of beautiful new friends on my business trips to South Africa. Derek and Louise were a young, newlywed couple from Durban; she was my local reseller of Internet security software, and he was the hottest surfer on Durban's beaches and a successful homebuilder. Our friendship blossomed quickly, and we had even started talking about organizing a fun trip for them to visit me in Toronto. But then, all of a sudden, the most unimaginable tragedy struck: Burglars broke into Derek's business one day, stole the little bit of cash he had just brought in to pay his casual workers, and shot both him and his father dead. Incredibly, my young and very strong friend was revived on the way to the hospital—but one of the bullets had gone through his spine and he was left paralyzed from the chest down.

I'll never forget how I felt the first time I went back to Durban after the accident to see them. I was afraid that I would be unable to do or even say anything meaningful, terrified of how I would feel when I was directly confronted with the heartbreaking aftermath of the attack. I feared that facing him and seeing the sudden and massive degradation in my friend's life quality would somehow absolutely wreck me, depress me, dim my energy and sense of optimism, crush my passion for life and make me live in a more paranoid way, in constant fear of losing what I had. And, instead of all that, I walked out of the airport in Durban and instantly fell in love with the magical powers of human love.

My good friend Derek was there, in his wheelchair, smiling from ear to ear—truly alive and loving life again because he wasn't alone. Louise was standing next to him, also with the biggest smile on her beautiful face, welcoming me to *their* new life. At the tender age of thirty, she had already completely embraced their new reality; she had infused him with so much of her optimism, she had wrapped him in so many meaningful layers of love and she was constantly discovering newer and more exciting paths for their new lives. I was utterly fascinated. I had never been so close to a human tragedy before, but I had also never had an opportunity to witness how miraculously the positive power of love can change lives.

Derek wouldn't have been alive if it hadn't been for their intense and real love; he wouldn't have been smiling, driving, picking me up from the airport, shopping, cooking, swimming, working (he had already reopened his business!), competing in disabled basketball leagues, travelling (they actually did end up making that trip to Toronto, just a year after the accident!) and even planning to have kids. Yes, kids! Within a few years of the accident, and after some fairly complex and creative IVF work, Derek and Louise became one of the first couples in South Africa to overcome such a severe disability and bring to life their own biological kids—our gorgeous twin goddaughters, Jamie and Donna Tromp!

In some ways the rich love lessons from my precious friendship with Derek and Louise helped me grow and prepare much more for the inevitable hard moments of life. When both my cool parents died young, it hurt a lot, but I found myself remarkably ready to manage. I knew how to be vulnerable as I leaned on Joe and how to let his love become my fuel for renewal. I was sad, but I could still smile, genuinely and a lot, about life. At the same time the experience of reflecting on their lives also taught me so much about how unconstrained love can become the driving force for a great journey. My cool and rebellious parents never held back, because they loved the journey a lot more than they loved that mirage of life that we often referred to as "destination." They didn't care if they ever arrived. They never became famous or wealthy. They just lived and loved every day. Their fulfillment came from loving, not from planning. They may have never rationalized all that, and they certainly didn't pass it down to us in words, but that's how they lived and that's why I think they died fulfilled. Without a doubt, I inherited their carpe diem genes—and I feel incredibly blessed for that.

life

My mother was taking a nap when I walked into the house, went to her room, tapped her on the shoulder and said, "Mom, I got suspended from school." She opened her eyes for a moment, looked at me, mumbled the words "That's okay," turned over and went back to sleep. And my heart rate quickly returned to normal.

A couple of days earlier, my outrageous mother had packed my bathing suit and told me to have a good swim on my 8th-grade school trip to some beautiful beach town. Swimming on school trips had been strictly banned all across Greece after a group of students had drowned in a horrific accident in the early 1970s. The teachers would always remind us and warn us before each trip. And the other kids' parents would also do the same thing—but not my rebellious and colorful mom, who loved swimming too much and loved bending the rules of life even more. She packed that bathing suit for me and set me up to be the chief rebel in my class that day. Eighteen of my friends and classmates ended up following me to some (supposedly hidden) beach not far from where the rest of the class was gathered for lunch and, of course, a little while later some of the teachers had found us there, frolicking in the water. There was nothing to deny; we all got suspended for three glorious days, including this supposed keener of a bookworm. Most of the others ended up having to face the wrath of their furious parents. I, on the other hand, simply watched my mother yawn, turn over and continue her nap!

That's how she was built, and those were the types of genes she apparently passed down to me. She interpreted rules, instead of following them. She prioritized life her way. She found and baked fun into every moment. She laughed a lot. And she loved pranks.

April Fools' Day was like Christmas in our home. We couldn't wait to outdo each other and to also gang up on everyone else outside of the immediate family. One year, when I was in high school, my mother drove us to an electronics store to buy the longest video cable available (I think it was twenty or thirty yards long). We ran it secretly from our neighbor's TV, through her window, across her yard and ours, through our window and into our VCR, retuned all her TV channels to the output frequency of our VCR, popped in one of my dad's porn tapes and simply waited for that lovely, elderly, prudish and allegedly virgin woman to come home. We all huddled by the front windows and watched her walk up from the bus stop. As she always did when she got home, she changed into her robe, sat down on her sofa and turned on the TV. Her screams were so loud that we could hear them through the closed windows. Moments later she was on the phone with my mother, warning her about those "bloody communists" who had started broadcasting this stuff to everyone's home because their mission was to destroy our society. My mom was my hero again that day!

I grew up surrounded by unspoken lessons on how to squeeze the most juice out of life. Ironically, as my parents grew older and stiffer and as they watched me perfect their teachings and exceed their rule-interpretation accomplishments, they worried a lot about me and tried very hard to pull me back—but it was too late. The journey from conscious or habitual blind obedience to "life optimization," as I think of it, was irreversible.

From the moment I left home, I was an optimizer. I invested my creative energy into figuring out how to fit as many of my favorite things as I could into my life. When I was in university and still had access to my dad's free airline passes, I would crisscross the world in the most impossible of ways, just because I could. I would leave Brandon at noon on a Thursday, take the bus (or hitch a free ride) to Winnipeg, hop on a flight to Toronto, catch a late-evening flight to London, jump on a connecting flight to Athens and walk into my parents' home without any warning early on a Friday evening. After thirty-six hours of partying with my old school buddies, I'd then travel another twenty hours to get myself back to Brandon in time for a good Sunday night's sleep, and turn up well rested for the following week's classes. Each time I flew on one of his passes, my dad would see a mere $8 service fee deduction of his paycheck—but the charges were actually adding up so fast that at some point he started to complain and threatened to start asking me for the money!

The more grown-up versions of my life-squeezing behavior may have been less physically draining, but they were just as intense and had just as much impact. From living in a penthouse condo that was worth almost ten times my annual pay and charging the monthly rent on my credit card so I could earn even more frequent flyer miles, to reselling all my records to my little brother as soon as I had recorded them onto cassettes, life always seemed full of great opportunities to stretch, innovate and make more out of every moment. Why not find a smart way to combine a full, or at least a fully productive, workday with a fabulous summer afternoon at the beach? (When the BlackBerry was first invented, I thought the world had finally been fully redesigned in my favor!) Why not figure out how to have a free live-in chef at home? And why ever miss a party, a vacation, a swim or a beautiful sunrise when all it took to squeeze them into my day was a creative interpretation of the rulebook?

My distant ancestors in Greece had a great saying about how appetite increases once you start eating. The list of my favorite things may have been short and simple when I was a kid, but it's grown a lot more complex and comprehensive over the decades. The slow crawl up Maslow's pyramid has shifted the balance away from the superficial and much more towards the meaningful and lasting, but the intensity and style of my pursuits hasn't really changed much. And while the taste buds may have evolved, some of the most basic, natural and simple satisfiers continue to rule the average day: sunshine, cycling, beaches, hikes, trips, spas, numbers, weather, spontaneity, great food and, above all, people. I can thrive on my own, and I often do, but I draw all my energy from spontaneous and often unstructured interactions with others. I love learning, and I adore teaching. Two of my most favorite and basic daily rituals involve reading the newspaper cover to cover and then clipping (once upon a time with scissors, now through screenshots on my iPad) and sharing articles, often along with my own comments, with Joe.

And of course, each year April Fools' Day still feels like Christmas!

work

In Greek, the words *slavery* and *work* sound almost exactly the same, and they're actually even spelled the same! While I have no expert opinion on whether the similarity in nomenclature may have somehow impacted the work ethic and productivity of average modern-day Greeks, I do remember growing up with a distinct aversion to working or investing any effort beyond the absolute minimum I could get away with. My summer jobs during high school were defined by an almost comical mix of resentment and creative cheating. I just couldn't fathom why I should waste beautiful, sunny summer days slaving away as the local plumber's assistant one year and as a production assistant at my uncle's cassette recording studio the next. And, more than anything, I couldn't cope with the structure, the routine and the predictability of it all. Why did I have to work until 5 p.m. each day? What good could possibly come from all those arbitrary rules? Why were they paying me for the amount of time and freedom I gave up to be at work each day, instead of paying me for what I produced? I felt uncomfortable and completely trapped in a box that made no sense whatsoever to me.

Things weren't really that much different when I got my first real job after university. My degree was in computer science and mathematics, so I went looking for programming jobs. A good friend of mine told me about a staffing agency that was hiring young programmers to place them on contract at the shiny new data center that Air Canada was about to open in Winnipeg, so I applied, and easily got the job. Here I was, twenty-one years old, with a sexy and easy new job as the youngest computer programmer in that Air Canada building, making remarkably good money but still feeling stuck inside a box that sucked away at my life. I got paid for being there, not for achieving.

I dreaded the routine, the slowness, the rigidness. Everyone went for coffee break together; everyone took lunch at the same time; then another coffee break; then that pathetic good-night they would all say to each other as they walked out of work, even though to me that moment always felt like the beginning of my real day—not the end! Paydays, assigned parking spots, meaningless department meetings, retirement parties—it all felt like prison. And of course there was no Internet back then and no such thing as surfing at work, so I invented another method of keeping my brain awake: I had access to all of Air Canada's operations reporting systems, so I would entertain myself (and feed my insatiable hunger for numbers) by analyzing their flight statistics, daily passenger loads, on-time records and—naturally—all their hourly weather reports from each airport.

I don't remember what faint hope I was hanging on to, or whether the wildness of my post–5 p.m. life dulled the pain and recharged me for the next day, but somehow I was able to keep going like this for a year and a half—and I might have lasted and rotted for even longer, had it not been for my very enlightened manager, who sat me down one day and talked to me about going back to school to broaden my career options. He told me everything I was trying not to notice at work each day; that I was too creative, too people-driven, too unstructured and too broad a thinker to be spending the rest of my career doing that type of "square" work. He encouraged me to find a way to get into an MBA school right away, even though I might have been a bit too young and inexperienced for some. I couldn't stop smiling. I thanked him, and thanked him again the next day, and I loved the way I felt: That square box was suddenly gone.

I quickly zeroed in on the only co-op MBA program in North America, at McMaster University. I had gotten used to making and stashing money, and I couldn't imagine it all draining away, so the idea of working some interesting jobs in between my academic terms was irresistible. I was told that getting accepted into that co-op program would be tough because I had so little work experience, but I managed to get in. Right after my twenty-third birthday, I packed up my piano, my boyfriend, my cat and my car and moved to Southern Ontario to start chasing the bigger dream.

All three of my MBA work terms were about as horrid as my programming job at Air Canada had been. Apparently those kinds of prison boxes didn't exist only in Winnipeg; they were just as common and miserable in Toronto. If anything, things were even duller for me, because I was now only a co-op student, and my employment by those large, amorphous organizations was more of a charitable act; nobody really cared if I contributed anything or if I felt useful in any way. Thankfully, they were all very short gigs—less than four months each—so at least I could easily count down the weeks and the days. But the other hidden benefit was that I now had a bit of experience, some interesting new connections in the world and a restless and vastly underused mind, so I was able to truly invent, pitch and design the perfect custom job that I would be able to plunge into as soon as I finished my MBA.

Here is how the pieces came together: Through my ultra-dull job in Winnipeg, I had gotten to know the guy who ran the staffing agency that employed me and, through him, I had learned a little bit about how that industry worked and how they made money. Conveniently, the agency was in Toronto, so I was able to develop and maintain a bit of a friendship with him through my MBA years. He was a very successful young guy, not that many years older than I was, and the contrast between our lives was a constant source of fascination for both of us, and an effective friendship glue. He had never gone to university, had focused all his energy on working and making money quickly, had married and had kids very young and seemed to always know exactly what he wanted in life. I had really worked for only a year up until my mid-twenties, I had no money, I had given up a well-paying job to go back for postgrad studies, I had no appetite to follow any kind of structured path in life but, beneath all that, I felt as hungry and as creative as he was.

So we started spending more and more time together towards the end of my MBA, and then one day I pitched to him what might have been the oddest concept he had ever heard: I asked him to hire me as his export manager. I told him about the Persian Gulf being one of the most expat-labor-dependent parts of the world, particularly in terms of technology jobs and especially with Canadians. I showed him how no other Canadian staffing firm had focused there yet and also convinced him that if he were to start advertising positions in the tax-free countries of the Gulf, he would generate tremendous interest among systems professionals in Canada and would dramatically expand his agency's database of candidates. And I also showed him how my salary and my travel and all of our other export development expenses would actually be covered by a fantastic combination of federal and provincial government programs that were specifically designed to encourage companies of his size to develop markets outside Canada. The facts were all solid, and the idea was as irresistible as it was totally off-the-wall, so we shook hands and decided to go for it. And I had finally created a real job for myself!

The ride was definitely outrageous and full of interesting lessons and surprises. We found clients; we advertised their job vacancies in Canadian newspapers; we completely flooded our database with new candidates (at some point a single Middle Eastern job ad in *The Globe and Mail* brought us more than 7000 resumés!); we learned how to manage cultural diversity of the most extreme kind and how to explain to Canadian women that they needn't even apply for such jobs in Saudi Arabia; and, above all, I learned how I was made to work creatively and differently.

I always stood out, no matter where I was: I was the different guy with that very different job when I was in our Toronto office; I was absolutely out of the ordinary, their ordinary, every time I sat in a meeting in Kuwait, or Dubai or Jeddah. The only regular thing about my work hours was jet lag. And the only reason I was earning an income was because I was building something, not because I was showing up at work. I couldn't get enough of it! While all my MBA buddies were working at banks and investment houses up the street, I was busy interviewing IT directors twice my age and warning them about such things as the beheading I had witnessed on my last trip to Riyadh.

I also quickly fell in love with exporting. It wasn't just the travel and the little bit of glamor; it was also the unconventionality of the work and the unusual survival and success skills that were required. I loved dredging up the six words in Arabic that my mom had taught me as a kid and using them to charm my clients. I thrived at doing deals over meals, instead of boardroom tables. I discovered the extremely important and inverse correlation between physical distance and emotional proximity: The farther you are from your clients and partners, the more you need to trust and respect each other in order to be successful. The unique emotional content of my job was sweet and gratifying— so when the Kuwait war happened in 1991 and our staffing work suddenly fell apart, I found myself at another company managing their exports overseas. Different company, entirely different products (we were selling data communications equipment) and much more established internationally, but the work was just as original and inspiring for me. I was making friends all over the world, defining my own recipes for success in different cultures, inventing new ways to harness the fantastic creativity of our Canadian trade missions overseas and always loving the thrill of being able to stand out, no matter where and how.

Then came a third export job, at a voice recognition software firm that was a little ahead of its time and soon went bankrupt, and a fourth one at one of the world's first Internet firewall companies. That fourth one was the wildest ride of all; we were trailblazing and working harder and faster than I had ever imagined, but I was completely absorbed by our success and by how fast I seemed to be growing, along with the company. I was still the guy with the very different job, and I still drew so much oxygen from being able to operate autonomously five thousand miles from home, but I was also enjoying a lot of the lessons that came with being part of a rapidly expanding business. Eventually, I opened our three little sales and support outposts across Europe, and I moved or hired our staff over there. I started to build a bit of a public relations function into our overseas work. And I also discovered the interesting feeling of being the guy with the most significant numbers, because so much of our company's revenues were coming from my European distributors, and so many eyes were trained on me at the end of each month. And I was still just in my early thirties, still a weird kid who preferred to talk about the weather and numerical coincidences.

At the beginning of 1997, I got a fascinating call from a headhunter: Maritz, the successful Canadian subsidiary of a large global marketing services agency, was looking to hire an executive to lead a new but fairly significant global division. A few months earlier, they had won a contract to manage all the incentive programs for IBM's 25,000 resellers and distributors across the world, a job that required setting up support centers across North America, Europe and Asia to manage hundreds of millions of dollars of IBM's marketing support funds and an enormous volume of exchanges and communications between all those resellers and giant IBM. They had been searching for someone who had expertise in channel marketing in the IT industry and had also worked extensively overseas. I suppose that was still a bit of an unusual combo at the time, so my name popped up, and I found myself interviewing for a job that was much bigger and very different from anything I had done until then.

I got the job within a couple of months and was suddenly swimming through the most significant, and at times most intimidating, transition of my entire career. The lonely cowboy of the wild, fast, but totally unsophisticated world of computers and technology was now sitting at the table in the executive boardroom of a global marketing agency. Only thirty-three years old and just a decade and a half off the boat, I had an army of older, experienced, smart people from all over the world reporting to me. This meant learning faster than ever before in my life, and at times, barely able to keep up, I felt a bit like Chauncey Gardiner in Peter Sellers's final movie! I thought I looked too young, acted too inexperienced and spoke in too unsophisticated a manner to deserve that kind of job, but in the end, my fear of being "found out" served as the best propulsion fuel: I thrived in the job, made a career home for myself and have since often referred to my Maritz years as my second and much more important MBA.

Apart from all the great work and growth, that chapter of my career also contained an unmatched level of glamor and fun. Maritz has always run some of the world's most coveted corporate incentive programs and we, as leaders in that organization, had opportunities to not only sample the goods but also, as part of our job, play host to some of our top-achieving salespeople on remarkable incentive trips. The experiences were truly amazing, and at some point Joe and I lost count of the number of helicopter rides we had taken in various corners of the planet. We saw extraordinary places; travelled in submarines, private limos, luxury yachts and seaplanes; enjoyed sensational meals; opened priceless bottles of wine; and slept in some of the world's best hotels. From the deepest jungle of the IT world to the refined and absolute peak of the marketing services industry in the blink of an eye! It was the most meaningful and perhaps most important step up in the career of this immigrant boy.

Then came the temporary but significant exit triggered by my young mom's very sudden death, which completely knocked me off my foundation. I woke up one day questioning the entire conformist rat race, and decided to exit my career.

And off I went. I felt inspired, strong, confident and smart enough to blow up all my routines in the pursuit of living a fuller life. I learned how to count breaths, smell flowers, really connect with my people and—more importantly than anything else—rank the most valuable elements of my life. That ranking exercise happened so fast that within six weeks of leaving my career I had already written that seventeen-notepad-page letter on that long, quiet night flight over Africa, and I knew exactly who was meant to be holding my hand through the journey of the rest of my life.

I took a whole year off. For twelve long months I invested energy in everything except my career. I didn't look for jobs, I didn't even have an answer for those who asked what I would do next. The whole conventional world around me doubted me and tried to talk a bit of sense into me. My dad couldn't comprehend it and eventually gave up asking questions. But Joe got it, loved it, quietly admired it and kept feeding my passion and courage to be different. He watched me grow through that year and knew that good things would come of it.

Even on the conventional side of life, really good things came from it. My next real job, after a couple of post-sabbatical consulting gigs, was my first experience at the CEO seat. Would I have gotten there if I hadn't stepped right out of the scene and taken that huge, year-long breath? I'll never really know that answer, but I'll never forget how "tuned in" and grown-up I felt when I was interviewing for the job. The executive table underdog of just a half a dozen years earlier had been transformed into a confident communicator who knew how to draw in smart people. My fear of being found out as the littlest guy at the table had been replaced by layers of unique pride and a solid sense of being fully in control: I was ready to sit at the head of the table and harness the brilliance of those who sat with me.

For the next few years, I ran Gorrie Marketing, one of the oldest retail marketing agencies in the country. It was an old shop, 125 years old in fact, full of piled-up legacy headaches and very hungry for new energy—and I was as odd a leader for it as the place was old. Going in, I had no idea how complicated and fascinating it would be to work as a hired-gun CEO in such a well-entrenched family business, nor did I realize how much creative diplomacy it would take to maneuver through it all each day. I had to immerse myself in three separate cultures at the same time; I needed to belong to the family, to some extent, in order to understand their anxieties and habitual priorities; I needed to "get" all the legacy attitudes and deep-rooted habits of the people who had been with that firm for a very long time, so that I could communicate with them convincingly in their own language; and I also needed to be seen as the passionate builder and driver of new ways of being and behaving at the firm. At any moment, in any conversation, whether with our people or with clients, I needed to be able to switch back and forth instantly and seamlessly between these three modes. It was a lot of work, particularly in the early months, and I found it utterly fascinating.

One of my most meaningful sources of support and growth during the Gorrie years was my new network of friends at the Young Presidents' Organization. I had always heard amazing things about YPO and had always craved joining it. The moment I took the reigns at Gorrie and finally qualified, based on my role and the size of the business I ran, I jumped in. It turned out to be one of the most transformative decisions I ever made, not just for my career but for my life in general and for our life at home as a family unit. I quickly learned that the main purpose of YPO wasn't to be a social club or a career-support group: it was to simply create opportunities for us to learn from each other and grow faster as both human beings and leaders in society. Our focus is a lot broader than just careers; we connect and share and learn in order to make ourselves better in every way: better role models in society, better builders of our homes and families; and, of course, more inspiring leaders for our people at work. The other remarkable thing about YPO is its fantastic balance between energy inputs and outputs: It's a volunteer organization and it comes with no preconceived requirements of the amount of time and energy each member should be investing, but the rate of emotional return for each of us is perfectly and directly proportional to what we put in. The more we offer into it, the more growth we get out of it.

And for a childless gay newbie member couple like Joe and me, it was very easy to plunge ourselves right into it from the start and reap incredible rewards from it. Being the first officially "out" couple in YPO Canada (out of more than 800 member CEOs), we definitely attracted a lot of attention. People started to invite us to lead events, speak about our experiences, meet and inspire their kids, take on more visible roles inside the organization and generally get more involved. We both had the time and the appetite. And the snowball kept growing. Within a (record short) couple of years, I had become the chair of the Toronto chapter. A year later I was the membership chair for Canada. I helped spawn some common-interest global networks, ran global conferences, and suddenly a big chunk of our social life had become wholly absorbed by YPO. It was an inspiring new chapter and, perhaps not surprisingly, it redefined the direction of the rest of my career.

green

On the last day of May 2007, I got on my bike and cycled all the way up to the northern fringes of Toronto to have lunch at the home of a man I barely knew. His name was Dean Topolinski and he was perhaps the best-known misfit in our YPO Toronto chapter. He worked out of his home, together with his brother who lived right next door to him; in fact, the two were so close that their houses shared one backyard and were essentially a compound for their two families. He did some very strange work; he owned a whole bunch of badly broken businesses that he had bought for pennies on the dollar, and his only project was to fix them up, in some cases even break them up, then dress them up and sell them for better money in the future. He appeared to be a gentle, warm soul, but people had already spoken to me about his huge "teeth" and his exceptionally tough negotiating style. He was definitely a polarizing member of our chapter; many loved him and some even went into business deals with him, while others didn't want to have anything to do with him.

I was excited to be going to Dean's, not only because of his spicy reputation but also because he had agreed to day-chair the most important and fun event of the following year for our YPO chapter. I was in charge of all our events for that year, so it was my job to make sure people like Dean knew what they were supposed to be doing and followed through on their commitments. So, in essence I was heading into a meeting with this controversial and somewhat legendary YPOer I hardly knew, and my mission was to "manage" him and to tell him what to do for us. The fact that he had offered to meet over a great lunch served by his live-in chef added a little extra horsepower to my northbound pedaling!

The beginning of our lunch chat was full of energy, fun and smiles. We had met only once before, and that was with a group of other YPOers, so this was our first opportunity to get to know each other one-on-one. The conversation was mostly about our personal stories, our spouses, his kids and our hobbies. We eventually ended up talking about the planned event and sorted it out fairly quickly. Then we finally got into a bit of business talk; it was obvious that I was fascinated by his unique work, and he seemed rather curious about how I had gotten to where I was.

A few months earlier, after a lot of coaching and handholding by some of my closest friends in YPO (my "forum mates," as we call them), I had mounted a complicated campaign to buy Gorrie Marketing. I had grown more and more restless with my job as a hired gun in such a family-intense organization, and I had solicited my mates' thoughts on how to make things better—or how to exit. Their consensus was that not only was I the right age and at the right stage in my life, I was also in the right environment and the right industry, and I had the right, energetic executive team to be able to buy out the business from the family. I was inspired and quickly got to work on it; I met with investment bankers, put together an attractive package, engaged my beautiful team in total confidence and pulled the trigger. Unfortunately, and perhaps not surprisingly, the family was not tempted by our offer.

I was left pondering my future and also helping my superbly loyal former teammates figure out new jobs for themselves. Obviously, we all felt disappointed that we hadn't ended up owning that business; and I remember also feeling a great dose of guilt for having pushed things as far as I did and causing so much upheaval in the careers of my most senior people. At the same time, the debacle gave me a newfound freedom and the mental space to create new ideas. And that's how I found myself sitting in my backyard one beautiful spring morning, dreaming up something so different and, as it turned out, so transformative for my life and career.

The spring of 2007 was, without a doubt, the peak of the "green frenzy" in my world. Al Gore's movie, *An Inconvenient Truth,* had succeeded in bringing conversations about climate change into the mainstream, and suddenly, all my fellow marketers across North America were scrambling to figure out how to paint their products, their companies, their jobs and their talks with as much green color as they could find. The trend was explosive and the tricks to riding that big green wave simple and obvious—a bit too obvious and a bit too "vanilla," I thought. It bothered me that everyone was doing the same thing, reacting the same way and simply relying on the intensity of their green color and the volume of their screaming in order to steal a tiny bit more of the spotlight from the next guy. It was too simplistic, ephemeral and myopic. At this rate, I thought, the whole green thing would become nothing more than another forgettable spike, another silly fad. Consumers would quickly tire of it and move on to something else that inspired them or at least caught their eye.

In the meantime, however, from looking at some market research, I was noticing something else that intrigued my climate-obsessed mind: The biggest influencer of consumer behavior was not the change in the eco-packaging of their favorite detergent or soft drink but actually the freaky weather outside! Billions of consumers around the world were beginning to respond to symptoms of climate change much more than to cheesy TV ads about cleaner-burning gasoline for their giant SUVs. And, of course, my secret advantage was that I understood much better than almost all my fellow marketers that the symptoms of climate change we were seeing in 2007 were nothing compared to what we would be seeing, say, a half dozen years later in 2013. I was enough of a weather geek to figure out exactly what the trend lines looked like and to know that, in terms of our weather-weirding, we were still at the very start of an incredibly steep, hockey-stick-shaped curve.

So if the worst (or most bizarre) was yet to come, and if it was true that those signals from the heavens had the biggest impact on the thinking and the shopping behavior of the masses, then it was safe to conclude that we were actually at the very beginning of a brand-new marketing megatrend. This green thing wasn't just another fad, like square-toed shoes or miniskirts. Almost all the big marketers in the world were seeing it and treating it like a fad that needed to be exploited as quickly as possible. Instead, I started to see a fascinating advantage for myself, because I understood that we were only at the start of something more fundamental, permanent and huge. And I started to think about how I could build a big, new idea, a new kind of business that would be designed to grow along with this emerging megatrend, instead of just trying to ride a short-term wave. I felt both fascinated by my little theoretical niche and grateful that my lifelong obsession with weather and climate had not been extinguished along the way.

Through my years at Maritz and a consulting stint at Canada's main frequent flyer rewards program, I had gotten to know the incentives and loyalty marketplace quite well. I understood why consumers were so responsive to smart incentives and particularly how popular and effective reward points were in a society like ours. So, in my scramble to invent the next big, long-term "green" thing, I came up with the idea of the world's first "green points" program.

I did a quick scan and confirmed that nobody in any of the leading markets in the world had yet created any kind of an eco-rewards program, one that would reward consumers only when they made environmentally responsible purchasing choices. The idea was so simple and the void so obvious that I actually began to worry a bit: Was I missing something? Could it be that nobody had come up with this before because, somehow, the economics would never work or the impact on consumer behavior would be negligible? And then, after I dug even deeper and convinced myself that there were no simple or obvious showstoppers and that I just happened to be the first weird, climate-aware business guy to think of such an idea, I began to worry about the length of my runway: With the market so obsessed with green, what if someone, somewhere else, was thinking of the same idea at the same time? What if they had more money and connections or much more of an existing platform to turn the idea into a real thing? What if I had just come so close to being an inventor of something, for the first and only time in my life, but wasn't quite going to make it?

So the tempo and the excitement went up rapidly. I began to sketch out a program, to try to figure out the real money and the opportunity behind it, the mechanics of it, and, of course, the market. Canada seemed like both the best and the worst place to try to do this. Best, because no country in the world appeared to be more points-happy than mine; Canadians were known to drive across town for a double-points special at the grocery store, and the consumer loyalty industry in our country was worth many billions of dollars per year. Worst, because all this success had created amazing entrenchment and consolidation among the leading players in this industry in Canada, so the prospect of being a tiny niche entrant in a space of very strong and wealthy giants was intimidating in the extreme. Plus, truth be told, although I may have always played and behaved and thought like an entrepreneur, I had never imagined myself as one—in fact, I was terrified of the idea. Me, on my own, building on such a big fantasy of an idea, starting a company, chasing billion-dollar customers and fighting off billion-dollar competitors? I couldn't fathom it.

But I certainly *could* imagine someone else doing something with my idea. The one thing I knew with total confidence was that my idea was hot, it was unique, it was perfectly current, and someone, somewhere needed to do something with it. I spoke with Joe about approaching the president of my old, beloved Maritz (a friend); or the president of Aeroplan, the frequent flyer program where I had consulted (an acquaintance); or the president of AIR MILES, the biggest points program in my country (also an acquaintance); and somehow figuring out a way to sell them my idea and have them nurture it and build it on top of their powerful platforms. I also spoke with some of my venture capital friends, the same ones who had helped me raise the money to try to buy Gorrie. No conclusive recommendations anywhere. Lots of fascination with the concept of a national eco-points program, lots of very smart questions, but no specific ideas on what to do with it next.

So here I was, in the middle of lunch at Dean's house, having interrogated him for quite a while about his businesses, and suddenly it was my turn to talk about mine. He knew that I had tried to buy my old company and failed, so his question had a bit more of a forward-leaning tone: "What are you working on?" I smiled, thinking that he might actually make a great sounding board and have some unbiased advice, because he was so removed from my industry. He was obviously a very smart and successful dude, so I asked him if he had the time to suffer through a bit of a download of a detailed idea. He responded very enthusiastically, so I invoked our standard YPO code of confidentiality and plunged right in.

Five hours later I was still at the table with him. It had been quite an afternoon. We had gone deeper and deeper into my idea; he had tried, very creatively but unsuccessfully, to punch all sorts of holes into it from every possible angle; I had thoroughly enjoyed the grilling; our tones and temperatures had gone way up at times; and in the end, here we were, doing something I would never have imagined as I was cycling up to his house earlier that day: We were actually shaking hands and agreeing to chase a wild new business idea together! In some mysterious and very special way, I had found my weird match: another misfit, another passionate nonconformist, another hyperenergized and energizing dreamer. He knew nothing about my world, my work, my successes and failures before, and I knew nothing about his—but, in a totally heretic way that would have made every conventional business leader's skin crawl, we were shaking hands on a downright crazy and fun new partnership. We would do this on our own: We wouldn't partner with the big boys, we wouldn't look to sell the idea—we would simply go and build a brand-new points program for Canada, and we'd do it in the most disruptive way possible. In a space filled with money and very wealthy competitors, we would pick the loudest and most visible David-versus-Goliath fights, on purpose, in order to quickly draw attention to our very cool idea. Dean's theory was that if the concept could inspire him, the most cynical and most unenvironmental business guy and consumer, then it had a lot of sticking potential out there.

So, on the 31st of May, 2007, magically and completely unexpectedly, Green Rewards was born. It had been conceived in my sunny backyard a couple of weeks earlier, and it was born through our amazing five-hour debate at Dean's dining room table that day. He would fund it; I would run it. We would follow our own, custom-designed method of turning on the risk tap one tiny step at a time; the more we assessed and confirmed, the more we would invest in it. And, for an extra dose of sizzle and inspiration for both of us, we built our beautiful fifty-fifty partnership on just a handshake and without a single piece of paper between us.

I still wake up, six years later, and think I was even crazier than my crazy mother—and I love it. What an unbelievable ride we had just launched ourselves on! Within a couple of weeks, we were already down in New York City, figuring out our technology providers for this monster we were about to build; within a couple of months, we had already hired half a dozen expensive, seasoned, sharp and well-known leaders from the industry; and by the end of the summer, there were articles in the newspapers, describing us as "the ones to watch." The tiny snowball grew into a full-blown avalanche in an extremely short time, just because we were both going about it in such an unconventional way, tickling and teasing the media with our dreamy ambitions, hiring prominent PR and branding agencies and charming some of the biggest Canadian loyalty gurus out of their boring and uninspiring jobs. We were the shiny new thing, and we were very good at getting more and more influential eyeballs turning our way.

By the end of that year, we had already built the team up to about fifteen dream employees, and we were in serious talks with one of Canada's largest banks about partnering on the launch of our country's first real environmental credit card. Things were looking great. At the Christmas party for our Green Rewards clients and partners (of course, we had to have a Christmas party already!), we found newspaper reporters snooping through the pile of nametags at the welcome table, looking for clues on who our launch partners in 2008 would be! And at Dean's family Christmas party a few weeks later, I found myself playing on a gorgeous baby grand piano that my eccentric and outrageously fun new friend had just bought that day, simply because I was going to be there. We were on such a crazy high and, beyond all the noise and the progress we were making with the business, we loved how our quirky partnership had also spawned such a deep and meaningful new friendship between us. At first it was just about the thrill of putting so much trust into a business relationship with a stranger, but then, over time, the bigger thrill was about discovering ever more layers of compatibility, vulnerability and powerful connections between the two of us.

Things got even wilder in the early months of 2008. Right around the start of the year, a couple of my young employees walked into my office to sound a mild alarm about a new, upstart green consumer marketing business that was also based in Toronto. While they weren't a loyalty points provider, their main focus was also on harnessing the momentum of consumerism in order to support environmental behaviors—and they seemed to be getting a remarkable amount of attention by the media, thanks to their charismatic and (apparently) fearless, young founder, who seemed to be charming every radio station and newspaper in the country. The little firm was called ClickGreener, and their concept was almost as simple as ours: If you did your online shopping by going through their portal, they would donate half of the affiliate fees they earned from all the major retailers to an environmental charity of your choice. Perfect win-win proposition for the average online consumer: Do what you would have done anyway, shop wherever you would have shopped anyway, but at least if you start your online journey through the ClickGreener site you'd be helping the environment in a meaningful way—without having to spend an extra penny. Again, they weren't really a competitor for us, but they were certainly generating enough noise in the media to potentially compromise our shiny position as the star green kid of Canada's corporate world.

We reached out to them right away and arranged for me to have lunch with their founder, Owen Ward. While for me this was just another lunch date, I learned later that for Owen, the buildup and the anticipation were almost unbearable. I didn't know it at the time, but Owen's little start-up was truly tiny; he was literally running it out of his apartment and, apart from the few hours his two minority cofounders were helping him each week, he was doing all this on his own. He was a young, beautifully energetic, genuine, warm, inexperienced and appropriately scared guy, who was suddenly being asked out to lunch by the much older CEO of one of the (supposedly) most prominent green businesses in the country. He consulted with his lawyer, and even spent time planning what to wear for such an important meeting. He showed up already feeling threatened and expecting some sort of intense and strategic assault. Instead, he found me fascinated by his brilliance and his genuine passion. I just couldn't get enough of him, and I remember exactly where I was—no more than twenty yards from the door of the restaurant on my way back to the office—when I had already dialed Dean and was telling him that we absolutely needed to buy this guy's business. I didn't really care about the business, and I knew we'd have no use whatsoever for the ClickGreener model—but I couldn't wait to join forces with the amazing Owen.

It all worked out perfectly. It took only a couple of dinner dates between Owen and me, and then a rather memorable trip for him up to Dean's suburban home office, before we had a deal. Now Green Rewards was made up of the two crazy founders, the fifteen or so fabulous builders and a new *über*entrepreneur, whose favorite sports in life were to disrupt, question, dream, stretch and care. Owen really cared: He cared about us, he cared about the real impact of the business, he cared about our clients, and he cared about the world. He wore his heart on his sleeve every step of the way, and he instantly earned the love of my entire team. We had the perfect dreamer among us, and it certainly made a difference through the rest of our unforgettable green journey.

Around the same time we moved into our shiny, new downtown Toronto office. In keeping with our wild trajectory since we had launched the dream, we picked a space that told a big, loud story about us. We took the former headquarters of a foreign bank in one of the most prestigious towers, and we looked (and felt) as if we had won the office lottery! Stunning boardrooms and offices, terrific address, lots of room for more growth and plenty of intimidation for those who may have thought of us as just another start-up. To add an extra dose of total eccentricity into the mix,

Dean decided to take that brand-new grand piano that had sat idle in his house since my drunken Christmas concert a couple of months earlier, and move it into our main office boardroom! I still relish the thought that we may have been the only firm ever, in the heart of the financial district of Toronto, with a grand piano right in the middle of its space. Our landlords and fellow tenants must have thought we were completely out of our minds.

And the crazy buildup continued. My colleagues were signing up dozens of remarkably eager companies that would provide fun and authentically green products and services as rewards for our millions of points collectors, once the program was up and running. Another team was creating partnerships with retailers who would begin offering our points to Canadians as soon as we locked in a credit card issuer (a big bank) and launched the program. And a third team was continuing to build our technology, our branding and our powerful launch plans. We had three very prominent (and expensive!) marketing agencies working with us, to help dress us up and get us ready for the big national launch. The monthly bills were growing larger and larger on every front, but so was our conviction that we were positively unstoppable and on our way to something great. The big loyalty giants had definitely taken notice and the chatter in the industry media was growing ever louder. A year into the journey we had become really good at broadcasting updates and provoking all kinds of reactions.

Somewhere around the one-year mark, I got a call from the wife of a good YPO friend. She was in charge of corporate marketing at BMO, one of our country's largest banks—and a direct competitor to TD Bank, with whom we had been dancing for the previous many months about the possibility of issuing a brand-new eco credit card that would offer consumers our loyalty points as a reward. It was an exciting call, because we would now find ourselves with a little bit of unexpected extra leverage in our discussions with TD. BMO had historically been very closely tied with the country's largest loyalty program (AIR MILES), so the call from my friend's wife was both very surprising and exciting. They obviously knew the loyalty game, and we knew that they were in contract renewal negotiations with the giant AIR MILES program, so our assumption was that they were exploring ways of deleveraging themselves a little bit from that dependence on a single loyalty points currency. We didn't hesitate for a moment, especially because we had been growing a bit impatient with our friends at TD, and we started to push forward quickly with BMO and harder with TD.

In the span of a couple of months, our landscape had changed entirely. Our conversations with BMO escalated exceptionally fast: once they figured out how tiny and weird and potentially unstable we were, they told us they would consider getting into bed with us only if they could also have at least some owner-ship stake in the business. We loved it, agreed to it, and suddenly there were many more people at the negotiating table. Then, as we worked through the numbers, their appetite increased further, and they started to discuss taking a majority interest in Green Rewards, instead of a small slice, and we continued to love it. Then their investment bankers concluded that it would make even more sense for them to simply buy the whole thing—and that's when we paused and contemplated things a bit more, because none of us had imagined becoming employees of a large, conservative bank. But the idea of gaining that much heft and prominence in the market (not to mention the crazy temp-tation of such an early exit!) made our hearts flutter, so we went for it. And, once again in record time, the bank had drawn up a beautifully tantalizing term sheet to buy our baby that was barely a year old and at that point had no revenues whatsoever. Dean and I were pinching ourselves; how could this be happening so quickly? Obviously, it made sense that BMO's contract renewal negotiations with the largest loyalty giant in our country were the driving force behind the rapid progress in our deal, but it was all still a bit hard for us to believe. And, armed with the confidence and excitement of a term sheet in our hands, we started to neglect our dialogue with TD Bank to the point where it just fizzled.

On the 19th of June, 2008—a date I'll never forget—I got a request for an urgent conference call with the most senior BMO executive who was driving the relationship and the acquisition deal with us. Maurice was one of the nicest, kindest and most straightforward people I had ever done business with. He had been with the bank for his entire career, and he was only a couple of layers from the very top of that huge organization. Normally, a deal of this size would have been well below his level, but he had taken a passionate interest in us and in me, in particular. At some point, after one of the long and complicated meetings with his investment bankers, he walked back into my office with me, closed the door, looked me right in the eye and said, "I hope you realize how proud I feel to be doing this deal with you, and I hope you know how envious I feel of everything you've been experiencing through this beautiful venture of yours." Without a doubt, this was one of the most meaningful, special and ego-boosting moments of my entire career—and I will remember it so clearly for the rest of my life. I already had such deep respect for that wise man, and he absolutely stole my heart with that one comment.

And now, I was being asked to make time for an urgent call with Maurice, ideally within the hour, so I knew it was something serious—and I didn't feel particularly good about it. I cleared my schedule, set it up and sat there with a million scary thoughts racing through my head, waiting for the clock to finally read 4:00 p.m., so I could dial in. When I did, Maurice was already on the line waiting for me. From the tone of his greeting, I already knew that it wasn't going to be a happy call—and it certainly wasn't. He was calling to inform me that, most unfortunately, our deal had been vetoed from "the very top of the organization," as he put it. He was unable to share with me the reasons for that decision, other than to say, over and over again, that it had nothing to do with my business, our prospects, our team, Dean or me. He sounded almost as distraught about the news as I felt— his misery was palpable even over the phone—and he promised that some day, over a drink or two, he would have the freedom to tell me the full story, which would hopefully make me feel a lot better. But he knew he was causing us a whole bunch of unexpected pain by pulling the plug, and he kept apologizing for it.

I was lost. I remember putting the phone down and feeling utterly paralyzed. My door was still closed, and outside it, all my amazing colleagues were waiting, hoping that I would come out to tell them it had been a false alarm. It was, after all, part of my job description to go out there and manage people's expectations and feelings and fears. But for perhaps the first time in my career, I was in too much shock to do what I knew I was supposed to. I couldn't get up. I couldn't even phone Joe. What would I tell him—that our cocky trajectory and behavior had brought us to a place where suddenly this livelihood project for us had evaporated in an instant? I simply could not face it. So, after ten minutes of staring at my screen and my phone and my hands and every other soothing and familiar element in front of me, I dialed Dean.

It may have been our shortest phone call ever. All he said was "I'll be right there" and, forty-five minutes and twenty miles of rush-hour traffic later, he was walking into my office and closing the door behind him. Obviously, I couldn't just sit there for all that time, ignoring my beautiful friends and colleagues outside that door. I gathered them all in the boardroom, and we had the big, honest conversation about the phone call with Maurice. They were as stunned as I was, but at the same time they seemed surprisingly bullish and strong. They asked lots of smart questions about our chances of reviving the defunct dialogue with the other bank, about whether the whole acquisition deal with BMO might have been an unimportant diversion from our real strategy, whether going back to Plan A and really going it alone might actually make us all a lot happier. In a moment of crisis like that, they seemed to cherish their existence as a dream team and their fun work even more than the prospect of a big, glamorous deal.

The first thing Dean did when he showed up was to give me a big, long hug without saying anything. Then he looked me straight in the eye and reminded me of our most basic motto, which we had repeated to each other hundreds of times since the start of our wild project: Friendship First! We had agreed from the beginning that the main benefit we both saw in our partnership was the birth and growth of a deep and genuine new friendship. The rest was secondary. And as soon as he jogged my memory and put me back in the right place, I felt full of positive energy again. Could we fix this mess quickly? Probably not—and perhaps never—but I was ready to try because, frankly, I had little to lose. I'd never lose him as a friend, and I'd never lose the tremendously rich memories of what we had created together, so everything else was less important. I had grown completely comfortable with the volatility and uncertainty of each week, and I was energized by every twist and surprise along the way. And that's all the call from Maurice was: another twist, another surprise in the most colorful career journey I could have ever imagined.

An hour after the hug and the chat with Dean, I was making another fateful phone call. I dialed Bryan Pearson, CEO of LoyaltyOne, the company that owned and ran AIR MILES. I had known Bryan through the industry, and more recently I had also met him as a newbie at a YPO event, so there was a new layer of comfort, confidentiality and trust I could invoke with him. I liked him. I didn't know him enough to say that I trusted him, but others had told me they trusted him a lot, and I had always found him to be very warm and easy to connect with. It was way past business hours by this point, still on that fateful 19th of June, so I dialed his cellphone and got him right away. He and I hadn't spoken at all in the thirteen months since I had started making all that green loyalty noise across the country, but that was understandable, and it didn't seem to make the start of our conversation awkward in the least.

I went straight for the kill, without holding back any facts: I told him about his biggest client having circled us for months and about having gotten to the point where they had completed a term sheet to buy us; I told him about the mystery of the deal evaporating so abruptly and for a reason that could not be disclosed, just a couple of hours earlier; and I offered to sell him the business on the exact same terms we had reached with BMO. He asked lots of questions on the spot, and we had a very open and superbly comfortable exchange about the business, the dream, the options, the go-it-alone versus not scenarios and so on. He told me he was personally intrigued by the possibility, asked for a few days to discuss it with his executive team and called me back three days later to tell me that we would try to figure out a deal. Talk about a roller-coaster ride!

In the midst of all that, however, there was one more enormous monkey wrench for me to manage: Dean's funding commitment for Green Rewards ran out. It had actually run out a couple of months earlier, but because the BMO deal was so close to being formalized, he and I had agreed that we wouldn't rock the boat and that he would continue cutting checks until we were signed with the bank. So the moment the BMO deal was scrapped, his (very significant, by this point) monthly checks also disappeared. No more payroll, fancy office rent, big agency payments or anything else at all. I was in an unbelievable bind, trying really hard to keep the whole thing together while also working to accelerate our LoyaltyOne deal as much as possible. Once again, the spectacular dream-team spirit was the highlight for me: All but one of my employees continued to smile and work as hard as they could. They knew I had never taken one penny in salary from the business, so they saw this new chapter as their turn to sacrifice a bit for the pursuit of the dream; they managed kids, spouses, mortgages and all sorts of other pressures and almost every one of them kept smiling proudly and doing great things through that weirdest of summers. And then, ten weeks after the last call with Maurice and just two weeks before the official start of the global financial meltdown, on the 2nd of September, 2008, we completed the sale of Green Rewards to the owners of the largest loyalty program in Canada!

dream

It was an incredibly close call. Our deal closed on the 2nd of September, and by the middle of that month the financial heart of the world went into convulsions. If something had delayed us by mere days, our publicly traded American buyer might have gotten spooked enough to back right out of the deal. The jitters had started some time before that. In fact, that was exactly why BMO had walked away from our original deal ten weeks earlier. When Maurice and I finally went out in mid-September for the drink we had promised each other during that fateful phone call, he was able to tell me that the bank had already known back in June what was coming, and that's precisely why we were vetoed right from the top. Money had stopped flowing for anything less than necessary, and our deal certainly fit only into the "nice-to-have" category. So, in many respects, we were unbelievably lucky to squeeze our closing into the very beginning of September, just before things really began to unravel around the world.

We spent the summer working on the assumption that Green Rewards, as a business, would be rolled into LoyaltyOne. We avoided exploring the more delicate question of whether the proposed Green Rewards loyalty points program would also get rolled into the AIR MILES program or whether we might still go ahead and launch it as a separate, competitive loyalty currency. That was a question for a later time; the more urgent decisions were about how to combine what I had built with the comprehensive organization that ran the AIR MILES program.

My first glimpse into the size and warmth of Bryan Pearson's heart was through the way he responded to my first call, on that scary evening in June, and the way he continued to respond throughout the summer; my second glimpse was through the way he supported the merger of the two teams. Half of my people became redundant and got packaged out, yet only one of them ended up being disappointed and turned litigious through the exit process (and even that was only because he was dealing with some self-inflicted career trauma from an earlier relationship with AIR MILES). All the others whose skills or roles couldn't be transferred over to LoyaltyOne walked away happy, proud and absolutely satisfied. And those who did make it across to the new company were made to feel welcome and given a remarkable amount of space to build their new careers inside Bryan's much larger shop.

Overall, there was so much openness and trust in the way Bryan interacted with me through the summer that, at some point, I ended up writing an article in our national YPO magazine in which I bragged about the flavor and tone of our deal. I wrote about the fact that, with so little need to look over my shoulder during those acquisition negotiations, I had probably learned nothing whatsoever—and probably set myself up to be far too naive if I ever had to sell a business again!

As soon as the deal closed, we began to work on the bigger question of whether Green Rewards, as a separate eco-points currency, should be launched at all or whether we should just take all of the cool assets we had built up and weave them into the powerful AIR MILES program. It wasn't an easy decision. By sticking with the original plan and still launching a separate eco-loyalty brand into the marketplace, we would be able to preserve its intended authenticity: It would be a true, green points currency, clean and simple as we used to call it, without the risk of being tarnished by any of the legacy image issues of AIR MILES. Even the greenest of greenies out there would trust it and embrace it. From an eco-authenticity perspective, this would clearly be the preferred scenario. But by blending it all into one and adding as much green as possible into the DNA of the existing AIR MILES program, we would be gaining something else of immense importance: scale and reach. With collector cards in almost three-quarters of all households in Canada, we could have a much more profound impact on consumer behavior across the entire country from the very start, by simply tilting the AIR MILES program more in favor of the environment. After much debate, involving a lot of people from both original organizations, we settled on full integration and, since our focus was so obviously on maximizing our impact, I acquired one of the strangest titles anyone had ever heard: Chief Impact Officer.

We set out to quickly prove the naysayers and the cynics (and there were quite a few) wrong. I hadn't just sold my soul and my business to the devil of consumerism; I had simply managed to get my hands on the largest steering wheel, one that could easily change the direction and the behavior of millions of consumers from coast to coast. If I had launched my green points program, I would have had to start from influencing just one consumer, the very first one that would sign up for our points, and then gradually grow from there. It would have been the purest and most wholesome loyalty points program on the planet, but it would have taken a long time for it to create real change in the lives of millions of consumers. This way, however, the only limit to our potential impact on the country was our own imagination and the extent to which we could tweak the AIR MILES brand without affecting its general appeal and power.

The first thing we did, before even touching the way AIR MILES points worked for the average consumer, was to green the company. Nothing could neutralize cynics and critics better than real, hard evidence of our investment in becoming a corporate beacon of environmental inspiration for others. So we started to roll out some big internal sustainability ideas that were truly original and ignited excitement and passion among our 1500 employees. We covered the large roof of our brand-new suburban call center with so many solar panels that we became the largest corporate solar energy producer in Canada! We installed a fleet of

Smart cars under our corporate headquarters tower in downtown Toronto, because we knew that many more of our employees would take public transit to work if they knew they could have access to a car during the day, in case they needed to leave the office for a meeting. And we kept going down that creative path. We avoided doing the conventional stuff and focused on the more innovative ideas that would capture people's imagination and make us the talk of the town. It all functioned beautifully, and the work was led by an original Green Rewards employee, who was brilliant at immersing herself into the LoyaltyOne culture and selling all these new concepts across the broader organization.

Then it was time to make some changes to the AIR MILES beast and the way it touched consumers every day. We started with the easy stuff: We took a look at the program's website, which is one of the busiest sites in the entire country. Millions of Canadians visit it every month to check their balances, learn about the latest offers at their favorite stores or redeem their miles for a reward. With such a vast, loyal audience at our finger-tips, why not tweak the site to make it a bit of an environmental guidepost for the majority of the nation? Why not gather content from some of the most trusted places in the country (the environmental NGOs, the government, even some of our giant retail partners), package it all up and then rebroadcast it to Canadians, almost like a free public service? It was easy to do, it cost us very little money and it earned us amazing accolades from even the strictest environmentalists. We created the one spot online where our fellow citizens could go and see aggregated information on how to renovate their home, what kind of car they should be driving or what were the most environmentally responsible choices they could make at the grocery store.

Our next layer of work involved the very essence of what we had been building back at Green Rewards: We gave Canadians a vast new range of much more eco-friendly rewards to choose from when they redeemed their miles. A lot of the core work had already been done by my old team, but armed with the heft and the name of AIR MILES, we were able to expand on it dramatically. For example, in addition to offering all sorts of eco-merchandise to our millions of collectors, we started talking to all the big public transit authorities; soon Canadians were also able to redeem their miles for transit passes in most major cities across the country. We even hired one of the best-known environmental accreditation agencies in the country to help us screen and rate all those eco-rewards, so that consumers never needed to doubt the authenticity of what we put in front of them. It wasn't just us, encouraging them to redeem their miles on some green product—it was a completely impartial third party endorsing that choice and explaining why that particular product was a better choice for the planet.

And then, finally, the last and most important layer of program greening was to start rewarding Canadians with more miles when they made more responsible shopping choices. This was the toughest project, because it wasn't entirely within our control. We had to work hard to bring along all our big clients, some of whom were actually a lot bigger than us, and show them how doing this together with us would actually help their business and their brand. And we had to orchestrate it all in a way that would be an impactful and significant event for consumers: We needed a lot of these big retailers to launch their eco-offers at once and, together with us, make a lot of noise about it across the country. It took us a whole year from the time the Green Rewards deal closed, but finally, in the fall of 2009, we went to market with a fantastic range of green bonus offers across Canada, together with our grocers, pharmacies, home improvement retailers, credit card issuers and others. It made a strong impact and, once again, made us the talk of the industry and of the broader media as well. For the first time anywhere in the world, consumers were earning extra loyalty points when they made the right environmental choices in their everyday lives; they earned bonus miles for buying the right food at the grocery store, the right wines at the liquor store, the right paints and cleaning products for their homes or even for switching from a paper credit card bill to an electronic one.

For me, that moment felt like the fulfillment of my entire simple vision, from when I was sitting in my backyard, wondering how to build something new around this emerging megatrend. In the span of two and a half years, I had chased the dream, built a crazy disruptor business, sold it to the biggest possible buyer and infected that buyer with all the right stuff that ultimately led them to launch the whole thing (in remarkable scale) across the entire country. I remember the first time Joe and I saw one of those AIR MILES TV commercials about being able to earn bonus miles with eco-purchases at a bunch of retailers—I felt like crying. I think most kids grow up wanting to become inventors, and that night, for the first time ever, I realized that I had somehow invented something.

While we were busy building and changing inside the big shop, the wild buzz that had started during the Green Rewards years was continuing to grow louder. It was actually a bit uncomfortable at times; I was still the favorite target of journalists, as the face of the greening of the program, but I was no longer an entrepreneur. Now, I was living inside a much larger organization that needed to contain me, manage me and even spread some of the fairy dust among some of my fellow executives. It wasn't working very well. Partly because I happened to be one of the earliest and more visible eco-entrepreneurs in the country (so the media would always specifically ask for me), and partly because it was hard to take the entrepreneur out of the boy and slow me down to the speed of a far more structured machine, there was usually a fair amount of tension on the PR front. I was still spending a huge percentage of my time giving speeches and interviews, writing articles, sitting on advisory boards and just spreading the story.

At some point, I was invited to a Canadian CEO council on sustainability and, as a group, we were going to spend a couple of hours with Prince Charles, who happened to be in Toronto on an official visit. The prince is, of course, one of the most outspoken and prominent environmentalists in the world, and he is particularly focused on big solutions with strong impacts. So when all of us around that large table introduced ourselves and told him how our organizations were contributing to the environmental sustainability of our country, he instantly zeroed in on my story. From across the table, he pointed to me and told the other, more prominent leaders in the room that they should study our example and "figure out ways to impact the behavior of the masses the way that gentleman over there is doing it with his points program"! As if that wasn't enough to stun me, he walked past my seat as he was leaving the room, gave me a friendly, light punch in the arm and said to me, in his perfect English, "Do keep me posted on your progress, will you?"

My friend Gerry Butts, who ran WWF Canada at the time and happened to be sitting next to me when this happened, turned to me and said, "Now that's an invitation to stay in touch with the palace, if I've ever heard one." And so I did, again to the bewilderment of my corporate communications colleagues. For the next twelve months, each time I sent a note and an update to the prince, I received a very warm reply. And then, totally unexpectedly, I received an invitation to visit him! He was hosting a group of senior corporate leaders from around the world to discuss a globally coordinated corporate strategy on climate change, and not only did he invite me to join that group (I was definitely the most junior person in the room, by a mile) but he also asked if I could come prepared to discuss the possibility of transplanting my Canadian idea to the U.K. The latter wasn't possible, because of course my idea was entirely owned by the operator of AIR MILES by that point, and the largest points program in the U.K. was owned by our most significant competitor, but I still enjoyed a terrific discussion with the prince's right-hand person on all the possible permutations and possibilities, and definitely enjoyed my day with the prince and the other corporate leaders, exchanging ideas on the broader topic of climate change. It was perhaps one of the most glamorous unintended consequences of my new eco-entrepreneur chapter.

Even before we sold the business to LoyaltyOne, I had gotten to know Al Gore. When he began to train people around the world as his authorized message spreaders, I approached him about organizing a special training session just for Canadian YPOers. The idea took a while to develop, and it was broadened along the way, but eventually I ended up bringing to him a group of YPOers along with a significant group of my Green Rewards colleagues, for his first-ever training session of Canadians in Montreal. That event made us the first Canadian business with more than one Gore-trained staff member. It was a standout claim to fame for us, particularly back then when the whole climate change discussion was still more like a debate. Making several of my colleagues authorized spokespeople on behalf of Al Gore was somewhat of a big deal. It was actually the Gore training that launched me into public speaking.

While I was running around the country, and sometimes to the palace in London, spreading our story and bragging about our accomplishments, a big surprise was brewing back in Toronto: An Ontario government department was contemplating the idea of using AIR MILES as an incentive for citizens to conserve electricity. It was an idea that one of my brilliant former employees, before I sold the business, had once created, and he had infected some of his government contacts with it. Up until then, the only two things governments could use in order to promote more responsible behavior among their citizens were advertising and cash incentives (rebates, coupons, discounts and so on). Advertising works, but it's never easy to figure out how well it's worked or who exactly has responded to a certain message. Cash incentives also work, but they're not efficient and, once again, it's difficult to figure out exactly where and how they've worked.

So my brilliant colleague approached an energy conservation authority in Toronto and proposed to them that if they used loyalty points as an incentive, they would not only save a lot of money (because they would be rewarding only those whose behavior truly changed) but would also gain a much clearer understanding of who, among their citizens, responded better to these types of offers; based on this, they could design future programs that were even better targeted and more efficient. The idea had percolated a bit at the beginning, but it died when I sold the business to AIR MILES, and the conservation authority assumed that we were no longer authentic enough for them to work with. Gradually, however, their appetite came back. They watched us transform the whole AIR MILES program in a very real way, they saw retailers offering miles to Canadians for shopping more responsibly and they started to think that perhaps it was worth trying that whole incentive concept after all.

So in the spring of 2010, just as I thought all my impact work at AIR MILES was done, and just as I had started contemplating my future somewhere else, we found ourselves launching the world's first partnership between a loyalty points program and a government! It turned into an incredible success: We took that agency's numbers from about 20,000 participants in its conservation campaign in 2009 (through advertising) to over 140,000 participants in 2010, while at the same time reducing their overall budget for the program by a stunning two-thirds! We quickly realized we were on to something remarkable, so we rushed and set up a brand-new business under LoyaltyOne: We called it "AIR MILES for Social Change," and its only mission was to deploy miles as incentives, mostly in partnership with governments, and reward Canadians when they made eco-responsible lifestyle choices—from taking public transit to conserving electricity, recycling, diverting hazardous waste and so on.

The opportunities were suddenly endless and the momentum was terrific: Our wild success with that first program in Ontario created an avalanche of calls and conversations from all over the country, and there was a time, in the early part of 2011, when we actually could not keep up with the work! In every single case, our results were spectacular. Sometimes things would go *too* well, and we would actually crash the websites of our government clients if a program required online participation by citizens (e.g., taking some type of awareness-building quiz or a pledge). In other cases, we would blow our clients' budgets in record time—because they hadn't anticipated so much participation and so many citizens to reward, so they would then have to scramble to unlock more budget while programs were still running. But invariably, the results ranged from great to off the charts, and we were off on yet another exhilarating ride.

And then came an even bigger and sweeter surprise: Barely a year into our success with government partnerships on environmental incentives, we got a call from a health department, wondering why they couldn't also experiment with the use of loyalty points as incentives to encourage people to eat healthier. We had not seen this one coming, and I personally felt a bit silly and embarrassed that we were being essentially out-innovated by a stodgy, old government agency. At the same time, though, I was thrilled at the opportunity, and we threw ourselves at it with plenty of passion. In June 2011, we launched the world's first healthy-eating incentive program across the entire province of British Columbia, in partnership with the B.C. government, the Heart & Stroke Foundation and the largest grocery chain in the Canadian West. Once again, perhaps not surprisingly by this point, the results were stunning. We were able to make a significant and clearly measurable difference in what kind of food people were choosing to pick up at the grocery store, just by dangling a few bonus miles in front of them.

That simple concept is anything but rocket science and yet, once again, we happened to be the first people to ever try it, anywhere in the world. And, just as had happened before, our initial success in B.C. opened up the floodgates for us across the country and across every imaginable form of health promotion. Canadians were suddenly being offered miles to exercise, to join programs to quit smoking, to take an online health quiz or even to engage with a health charity such as Heart & Stroke. The ride was even wilder this time, and by the middle of 2012, more than 70 percent of our new business was coming from the health promotion side. The same amazing Owen who had been with me since our humble early days at Green Rewards was now in charge of our health promotion work, and his energy and genuine passion was the biggest force behind the explosive growth of that business.

As we became ever more entrenched in areas of public policy, I found myself developing some very interesting and rewarding relationships with big public policy thinkers. This was different and much deeper than our early glamor days with the likes of Al Gore, David Suzuki and Prince Charles. All of a sudden, we were being invited to think and help develop transformative ideas for our nation along with politicians or very senior bureaucrats. I had always been fascinated by political and policy leadership but somehow never imagined myself being so close to that world. Now though, I was meeting mayors and premiers and ministers. The deputy premier of Ontario at the time, George Smitherman, who had once been skeptical of our ideas, gradually became one of our most outspoken fans and, eventually, a good personal friend. David Collenette, one of the best-known elder statesmen of our federal political scene, also became a terrific supporter, a formal advisor and a great friend. And Justin Trudeau, who was introduced to me by my friend and former green partner Gerry Butts, became an amazing partner in public speeches about social change and a unique friend who constantly inspires me to dream bigger and conform even less.

There is a very special story about how Justin and I first bonded: When I moved to Canada, his dad was still prime minister, and he quickly became a powerful role model for me. I would watch him on TV and read about him and try to follow his thinking and his style. I wanted to grow up to be just like him— smart, edgy, unique, funny, dismissive of fools, courageous and definitely quirky. Without knowing much about marketing and brand building back then, I admired how he had been able to craft and maintain such a sharp and unique brand for himself. I was so fascinated by his leadership style that, when I grew up and became a bit more successful and connected, I started to try to find ways to meet him. By then he was a very old man, living in Montreal, but I still wanted to sit down with him and simply thank him for all the inspiration, as well as for having helped create such a beautiful, welcoming, cool, modern and inclusive society for me here. So I worked at this little plan, talked to a few people who were somehow connected with him, but just as I got close to making it happen, he died.

I was so upset on the day he died that I actually sat down and wrote him a letter. It was a cathartic little note, and I titled it "*Au revoir*, dear teacher and friend I never met." It was the thank you I never got to say to him in person. That letter wasn't really meant to go anywhere—I just wrote it to feel better and then put it away. But one day, much more recently, after I happened to mention the story and the letter to my friend Gerry over lunch, he asked me to send it to him, and then he forwarded it to his best friend, Justin Trudeau! To my amazement, Justin called, said he wanted to thank me for how I had felt about his dad, told me he wanted to come and meet me—and a whole new friendship was born.

Back at work, in a fascinating way, AIR MILES for Social Change had become our little entrepreneurial venture inside the big corporate walls of LoyaltyOne, almost like an accidental granddaughter of my original Green Rewards venture. We were on a wild growth path and drawing a lot of inspiration from each other. My "tribe" of world changers had been growing steadily and in unique ways. Nothing about us was ordinary, least of all the way we kept finding and adding talent. Every time we stumbled across remarkable people—from young Georgia, who was interning at a climate change law firm; to young Jordan, who had invented and built an eco-exhibition business out of his university dorm; to young John, who could not reconcile his mainstream financial career with his geeky passion for climate change—we simply figured out how to fit them into our little army of change, even if we didn't exactly know what they could do for us at first. We became a team with the perfect blend of passion, experience and powerful cohesion. Our clients, our partners, our friends in the NGO community and even our siblings in the other LoyaltyOne businesses marveled at our distinct ability to think, imagine, talk and move as a superbly connected unit.

But as we grew to become so unusual and independent, it became too easy for us to forget where our social venture actually lived. We were the fastest-growing business unit inside our billion-dollar parent; we behaved so autonomously and had been cultivating such a special, separate brand for ourselves that it was becoming increasingly difficult to fit us properly inside the bigger corporate shell. We had labeled ourselves a "social venture," and our newly earned freedom was allowing us to branch out ever further and discover even less conventional sources of revenue—generating even more impact, of course. But this level of cultural distance from the mothership was also starting to create a good deal of tension. Large organizations, by definition, require conformity and predictability in order to be able to operate smoothly. Our little dream venture and the creative entrepreneurs it nurtured were definitely not great examples of conformity or predictability. We thrived on chaos, speed, surprise, disruption and boundless innovation. The mothership—particularly because it had always been a highly profitable and stable shop and needed to stay that way—had developed a solid, steady and very safe culture.

Eventually, with the arrival of a new president at our parent business, it was time to figure out how to make our venture behave a lot more like the rest of the organization. The logical way to do that was by reducing its autonomy and properly fitting it into the parent business. It had obviously thrived and grown as rapidly as it had by being on its own, but there was a healthy and very reasonable debate over whether it needed to retain its unique status. Being brought into the main organization meant that it would no longer even need a president—especially not this incurably nonconformist entrepreneur—so it was time for my exit. Just over four years after my initial beautiful deal with Bryan, Dean and I found ourselves selling our remaining interest in the business—and suddenly my corporate residency days were over. I found the separation experience more challenging than I had imagined. There was something about leaving my firstborn, the one and only invention of my entire life, that was remarkably sad; this was the way a mother must feel when her kid grows up and moves out. But, at the same time, I felt free again. My years as an accidental inventor and entrepreneur had taught me a great deal about my ability to create and build and drive—all of which would always be very difficult to recreate inside a safe and cautious corporate environment. It was time to dream of wild new things again.

It didn't take long at all. The moment I was out, a group of wise, keen and well-connected friends coalesced around me and started to talk about creating an international version of my old dream. If we had such terrific evidence from Canada that smart incentives could accelerate the adoption of public policy on a mass scale, and if I no longer had corporate constraints about replicating the idea elsewhere, why not find a way to do what Prince Charles had asked me to do three years earlier? That new chapter of the dream is only being written now, just as I'm writing this book, so perhaps the story will be covered in the sequel . . .

But, then again, maybe I am being too conventional by simply expanding on an old pattern instead of creating something new. Maybe the biggest lesson of the dream journey of these past half dozen years is that I have a lot more changemaker and inventor potential in me. Maybe simply replicating my social change incentives idea in country after country would be lowering the bar of my own creativity. Now that I've tasted it, I am aware of my capacity to dream and inspire real change for the world—and so the possibilities are tantalizing. Justin once asked me if I would run for office with him; I took a look at running an environmental NGO; I am enjoying writing this book; and I love the fact that there is no pattern, no specific path ahead, and there are no expectations whatsoever. There may be much more to come!

age

When I was a toddler I would start crying as soon as I heard the spoon hit the bottom of my dinner bowl—because that would be the first sign that whatever great meal I was enjoying was about to end.

When I grew a little older, I noticed that I preferred westbound flights, because when you fly west and chase the sun, time practically stands still, while on eastbound ones, time flies by twice as fast. I never liked it when an entire day would essentially vanish off the calendar because I was flying east, but I cherished those super-long days of flying from Athens to London to Toronto to Winnipeg and then taking a bus to Brandon. Twenty-four hours later, it would still be the same day.

Time has always been my most anxiously guarded asset. My numerically charged brain has never stopped feasting on the value, the beauty and the scarcity of it. I've never been able to live without a watch, and I've never been able to tolerate all those age-neutralizing clichés: "You're only as old as you feel," "Age is just a number" and so on. I know, I feel, I understand and I appreciate age in ways others find bizarre, fascinating, tiring and (most often) annoying.

I am creating this little memoir on the numerical midpoint of my adult life. Even though the number itself isn't particularly pretty or meaningful, for some time now I've been seeing fifty as an immensely significant milestone. There's all the great stuff about being at the peak of life, about the magnificent combination of energy and perspective and about the blend of endless opportunities and freedom. But, mathematically speaking, this is also the first time that the big spoon will start hitting the bottom of the bowl. Life should start feeling like an eastbound flight, and my calculator brain should obsess over the realization that there will soon be less runway ahead of me than behind me.

My age-defying and radically nonconformist mother dropped dead without warning at sixty. I was devastated by not only the enormous shock of losing her but also the illogical but uncontrollable realization that my reverse clock had just been started. I could practically count the days until I would reach that same age, and I almost started assuming that my natural expiration moment might be the same as hers. But the abrupt introduction of a deadline also imbued life and time with a beautiful new preciousness. Suddenly, each day had to matter; it wasn't good enough anymore to just wake up and live an ordinary day. Instead, the fast-ticking clock made it essential to maximize the fun, the human connections, the love and, above all, the impact.

Impact. The notion of it went from somewhere deep in my subconscious to the very top of my mind and parked itself there permanently. It became synonymous with wealth: If I have the ability and power to touch, influence and change something that matters in the world around me, then I feel rich. It may have been easier in my younger years to merely exist, enjoy, observe and learn, but it feels as if life became meaningful only when I grew up enough to be capable of really influencing others. From being able to hold the hands of those I teach and mentor to having the power to create businesses that defy paradigms and bring real change to our society, my grown-up definition of wealth is remarkably different from anything I used to imagine before. Now, that reverse clock isn't as intimidating, and the daily search for meaning isn't nearly as anxious. Time and its ugly, modern sister, money, no longer dominate me the way they once did. I am no longer expected to "arrive"; it's the journey, my very own particular journey, that provides all the fulfillment. And life is so much more beautiful this way.

One of the greatest side effects of this healthy shift of attention from the destination to the journey was the arrival of a very sweet, new friend: nostalgia. Immigrant, escapist and misfit boy didn't have any time or need for her before. Sure, she would tease me once in a while—the occasional smell of a fig may have reminded me of Monemvasia; I may have caught a glimpse of a country road that brought a flashback to those crazy student road trips in Manitoba; and the sound of my dad's voice on some old cassette may have triggered a brief burst of emotions. But those were fleeting little memories, and I didn't really know what I was supposed to do with them. They were simply there, and they were already mine anyway, so I just kept leaving them on the shelf. But then, when life started to change from a race to a project, all those memories became amazing assets, and deep, genuine nostalgia suddenly became a powerful force and a real enabler for me to inspire and change others.

I had an enormous bank account of diverse experiences to draw from: life on two very different continents; half a dozen bizarre micro-careers; exposure to some of the leading minds of our world; a brilliant brother with Asperger's; and a twisted, unconventional, uncomfortable and restless mind of my own. The rich cocktail of my life had real value, because so many parts of it could be dredged up to enrich conversations, guide ideas, inspire new forms of trust or simply add a lot more flavor and depth to life. I found myself reconnecting more meaningfully with my people back in Greece; helping my incredible little brother figure out why and how he's so different; building a deep and real bond with our only surviving parent, my beautiful mother-in-law; going on dinner dates with my wise old high school teacher; and writing this book. It has all made me feel richer, more useful, definitely more influential and immeasurably happier.

The peak of life is an extraordinary place. I don't feel tired, even though I've covered much more distance than I would have expected. I don't feel old, even though I'm always surrounded by much younger, real friends. I don't feel bored or anxious, even on days or weeks when I may seem to be doing or changing very little.

I don't feel scared or isolated, even though the only way I know how to create change is by disrupting. And I don't feel egotistical, even though I lead and influence in very personal ways.

My biggest asset now is my age, because of everything that comes with it. I truly have no idea what the second half will look like, but I feel a thousand times stronger, wiser, more self-aware, more needed and perhaps even more curious and adventurous than I did all those years ago on that first one-way westbound flight to Canada.

change

I wrote this book to help inspire more change for our world. I was raised believing that I needed to change in order to fit into the world, but I didn't really grow up until I realized that the opposite was true: the world needed me to help change it a little bit.

Everyone is a misfit somehow. I just happened to be born bolder, louder, quirkier and with more jagged edges than most. Fitting into an organized human society, respecting the boundaries of others, learning how to be understood and how to grow along with your tribe—those are all essential elements of survival. But the balancing act is much tougher for those of us with the more extraordinary gaps and skills, because it's so easy for us to go overboard and get ourselves squished into crippling conformism, shyness and self-doubt.

I could have ended up living in a suburb of Athens as a completely repressed homosexual man, married to a woman and raising beautiful children. I could have had a simple and easy career as a math or piano instructor or as a computer analyst. And I could have still been enjoying a predictable paycheck by keeping my head low inside the multi-billion dollar firm that bought my social venture. Any of those scenarios would have been "normal" and "good," according to some, perhaps even easy, but would have wasted a huge slice of my genes and capabilities. My raw story in this book is intended to inspire others, particularly those who were born a little more different, to test their boundaries and figure out a more daring and creative balance between belonging to society and reshaping their world, *our* world.

I haven't created all that much change in our world yet, but at least I have established a trajectory, and that gives me plenty of confidence about what's to come in the second half. It took me a very long time to grow up and understand what I could do differently and how I could draw others in. I may have looked like a disruptor when I got caught swimming on that school trip or when I was inventing my first job, but deep inside I was always really shy and scared. For far too long I felt too different, too hampered by my inability to fit in properly and too lucky to be sitting at that executive boardroom table or to be loved by the world's most genuine spouse.

I now feel proud and hungry. Proud to be infecting thousands of young people with stories about the thrill of disruptive change, the importance of harnessing unique genes and skills, the joy of being driven by uncompromising conviction and the real wealth of passionate leadership. And hungry, deeply hungry, for the snowball effect that's only just started. Now that I know who I am and how I can find my own unconventional route to the next peak, now that I've figured out how to see the world through my very own creative lens, now that I'm not afraid of labels and unreasonable rules, I can shape bigger dreams, rally bigger thinkers, disrupt bigger paradigms and create a lot more meaningful change around me.

author

Social entrepreneur Andreas Souvaliotis was the founder of Green Rewards and co-founder of AIR MILES for Social Change, and his achievements in influencing and rewarding behavior change on a mass scale have been recognized by social responsibility leaders around the world. A well-known writer and public speaker and an active member of the Young Presidents' Organization, Andreas is a leading Canadian advocate for climate change awareness and health promotion as well as for innovative approaches to social change. He holds a bachelor of science and an MBA degree; is a classically trained musician, avid cyclist and global citizen; and lives in Toronto with his partner, Joe.